C000042168

4-WHEEL DRIVE

HAMLYN

London . New York . Sydney . Toronto

4-WHEEL DRIVE

Julian MacNamara

Introduction by **NICK GEORGANO**

Four Wheel Drive was designed and produced by Campbell Rawkins
The Old Power Station, 36–37 Hamilton Rd, Twickenham,
Middlesex, England.

Designed by Peter Matthews

First published by The Hamlyn Publishing Group Limited
London . New York . Sydney . Toronto
Bridge House, Twickenham, Middlesex, England.

Copyright © 1985 Campbell Rawkins.
All rights reserved. No part of this publication may be reproduced,
stored in a retrieval system, or transmitted in any form or by any
means, electronic, mechanical, photocopying, recording, or
otherwise, without the permission of the Hamlyn Publishing
Group Limited and the Copyright holder.

Typesetting by Ace Filmsetting Limited, Frome, Somerset, England.
Reproduction by Chelmer Litho Reproductions, Essex

Printed in Italy

ISBN 0 600 34745 1

CONTENTS

INTRODUCTION

Four-wheel drive is almost as old as the motorcar. The first example came from the fertile mind of Ferdinand Porsche, and was one of his earliest designs. In 1900 he began to work for the old-established Viennese coach-building firm of Jacob Lohner, for whom he designed electric cars powered by motors in each front hub. It was a logical extension of this idea to use these hub-motors on the rear wheels as well, and this was put into practice on a curious-looking, semi-streamlined machine which saw the light of day at the end of 1900. It was named *La Toujours Contente* in response to Camille Jenatzy's famous land speed record car, also electric but not four-wheel drive, called *La Jamais Contente*. Only one was made, but Porsche was to return to the four-wheel drive theme with some enormous artillery tractors during the First World War. The principle of electric motors in each wheel was used by some American makers of heavy trucks in the early years of the twentieth century, either powered by batteries or using the petrol-electric system whereby a petrol engine drove a dynamo to produce electric power.

Four-wheel drive was mostly applied to trucks in the early days, but a notable exception was the Dutch-built Spyker of 1904. This not only had drive to all four wheels by shafts running fore and aft from the gearbox, but also a six-cylinder engine, one of the world's first, four wheel brakes and a Vee-radiator. The 8.7-litre engine developed 60 bhp, and there was talk of the car being entered in the 1904 Gordon Bennett Race, but it never reached the starting line. However it did make the fastest time of the day at the Birmingham Car Club hill climb in 1906. Only one car of this size was made, but thee or four 32/40 hp, four-cylinder models were built and sold at £960 each. They were reputedly popular in the Dutch East Indies where they were better able to cope with monsoon-damaged roads than two-wheel drive cars. However this was not enough of an advantage to justify their high price and complexity of design, and Spyker built no more.

Most four-wheel drive cars, from the days of the Spyker up to the present, have used a single engine and a transfer gearbox to take power to front and rear axles; not so the extraordinary 'Double Ender' racing car built by John Walter Christie in 1905. This had two 60 bhp engines, one driving the front wheels and another, behind the driver, powering the rear wheels. As with all Christie's cars, the wheels were driven directly from each end of the crankshaft, which took the place of an axle. There was no gearbox or differential. When the engines could be persuaded to perform in unison, the Double Ender had a good turn of speed, and managed to cover a mile in 38 seconds, equivalent to 99 mph, at Ormond Beach, Florida.

Needless to say it was not a production car, and Christie took the rear engine out when he entered the car for the 1905 Vanderbilt Cup. The double-ended principle was revived much later by the German Tempo company.

The first commercially successful four-wheel drive vehicles were trucks made by the Duplex Power Car Company of Charlotte, Michigan. The first was a three-quarter-tonner powered by a 20 hp, two-cylinder engine under the driver's seat, with internal gear drive to all four wheels. This appeared in 1908, and within a few years a larger two-tonner appeared, with a four-cylinder engine under a frontal bonnet. Further west, in Clintonville, Wisconsin, blacksmith Otto Zachow and his brother-in-law William Besserdich made a four-wheel drive steam car in 1908, following it with a larger petrol-engined tourer which they named the Battleship.

About ten of these cars were made, powered by 55/60 hp four-cylinder Wisconsin engines and selling for $4500. They coped well with the snowy conditions of Wisconsin, and also with the mud which filled the roads when the snow melted, but the high cost put most buyers off. The Four Wheel Drive Auto Company might have joined the ranks of countless other ephemeral American car manufacturers, had not a Battleship which was touring the southern states attracted the attention of Captain A. E. Williams, purchasing officer for the US Army. He was organising an endurance run to evaluate motor vehicles for adoption by the Army, and invited the Four Wheel Drive company to enter a car. Dubbed the 'Nancy Hank' the vehicle outperformed the competition in a gruelling month long test run, so well in fact that the company was commissioned to supply four-wheel drive trucks, which became known as the B type. This was powered by a 56 hp, four-cylinder Wisconsin engine, which drove through a Hele-Shaw multi-disc clutch to a three-speed Cotta gearbox with an integrally-built transfer case. This incorporated a central differential from which drive was taken by shafts to the axles, on each of which was an ordinary differential. To prevent all the power going to one axle on soft or snowy ground, the central differential could be locked to provide equal power to each wheel.

Production of the Model B began slowly at first, with only 18 trucks delivered in 1913. With no hostilities in prospect, the Army was not going to indulge in lavish orders, and the civilian market was not sufficiently convinced of the advantages of four-wheel drive. All this was to change within a few years – General Pershing's Mexican campaign led to orders for 38 Model Bs, and, even before America entered the First World War, FWD and other US truck makers received large orders for vehicles to aid the British and French war effort. Demand for the Model B was so great that the Clintonville factory could not cope, so the design was farmed out to other manufacturers such as Kissel, Mitchell, Peerless and Premier. Production continued to about 1925, by which time more than 16,000 had been made, including 700 in Britain, where the makers were known by the splendid title of the British Four Wheel Drive Tractor Lorry Super Engineering Company Limited.

The other name which made four-wheel drive famous in the First World War was Jeffery. In 1913 the US Army Quartermaster Corps paid a visit to the factory of the Thomas B. Jeffery Company at Kenosha, Wisconsin, which was already supplying conventional light trucks to the Army. As a result of a request for a truck capable of off-road work, Jeffery's engineers came up with the Quad, a two-ton forward control truck which not only drove on all four wheels, but steered with them as well, giving a turning circle of only 45 feet. Four wheel brakes enabled the Quad to stop in its own length from its top speed of 20 mph. Like the FWD, the Jeffery Quad first saw service in Pershing's Mexican campaign, where the US forces were engaged by Pancho Villa's troops over trackless terrain. Here four-wheel drive proved its worth, being able to negotiate scrubland and gullies which inevitably defeated the ordinary vehicles. Wartime production of Quads was farmed out to three other factories, Hudson, National and Paige, and in 1918 a total of 11,490 were made, at that time the greatest number of trucks ever built in a year to one design. They continued to be made after the war, fitted with oil tanker, tipper and fire engine bodies as well as ordinary sided trucks. When production finally ended in 1928, more than 41,000 had been made.

The First World War created a need for better traction in Europe as well, though nearly all the vehicles made were tractors for pulling heavy artillery rather than load-carrying trucks, for which the French and British armies relied on American machines. In France, Latil, Panhard and Renault all made 4×4 tractors, while the German and Austrian armies were equipped with enormous tractors made by Austro-Daimler to Porsche designs, and also by Magirus and Büssing.

With the coming of peace, interest in four-wheel drive dropped sharply; few new designs appeared in the 1920s, though FWD in America and Latil in France improved and perfected their trucks and tractors. In 1923 the British Royal Army Service Corps assembled an artillery tractor based on captured German vehicles, which they named Hathi (Hindustani for elephant). An improved version of this was made by Thornycroft, powered by a 90 bhp, 11,197 cc, six-cylinder engine with a gearbox offering six forward speeds and two reverse by means of an auxiliary gear train. The Hathi could haul a ten-ton load up a one in five gradient, and exert a pull of 9000 lb through a winch. Because of lack of demand for military vehicles at the time, only 24 were made, but they gave useful service in India and Australia for many years. A 6×6 version, of which only one was made, was the first British six-wheel drive vehicle. An interesting Italian design was the Pavesi tractor, which had a frame articulated in the centre to keep all wheels on the ground. The prototype was built in 1914, and various models were tested during the inter-war period, and licences sold to foreign countries. In Britain Pavesi-type tractors were made by Armstrong-Siddeley.

Away from the military sphere some interest in four-wheel drive was shown by racing car designers, whose aim was to transmit as much power as possible to the road without wheelspin. In 1932 Ettore Bugatti announced his Type 53, which used the 4.9-litre twin overhead cam straight-8 engine of the Type 50 in a new chassis with independent front suspension (the only Bugatti design to do so). The gearbox contained a differential, and drive was taken to the front wheels by a shaft to the nearside of the engine. The propshaft to the rear axle was also offset to the nearside. It was said that the car would compete in races, but in fact the two built were only seen in hill

climbs, and from the choice of gear ratios it would seem that they were planned with hill climbing in mind. Louis Chiron broke the record at La Turbie in 1932, and René Dreyfus broke it again two years later, exceeding 100 km/h (62 mph) for the 6.3 km (four-mile) course for the first time. After this the Type 53s were not seen again in competition, though one still exists in France.

The other exponent of four-wheel drive in racing was the American designer, Harry Armenius Miller. He had made front-wheel drive racing cars since 1925, and in 1931 he built an unsuccessful four-wheel drive V-8 for the Indianapolis 500 Mile Race. In 1938 he was commissioned by the Gulf Oil Company to design a completely new car; this had a rear-mounted, three-litre, six-cylinder engine developing 246 bhp at 6500 rpm. The 45-degree inclined engine drove all four wheels through a four-speed gearbox. Four of these cars were made, and although they ran at Indy in 1939, 1940 and 1941 they never completed a race. In 1940, after one car crashed and was burnt out, the other was withdrawn by order of the officials who thought the frame-located fuel tanks were dangerous. However one of the Gulf-Millers did set a dozen international records at Bonneville Salt Flats, including a flying five kilometres (three miles) at 158.446 mph. In 1938 Miller designed and built one four-wheel drive roadster powered by a V-16 engine, to special order.

The 1930s saw a tremendous growth in light four-wheel drive vehicles, practically all of it stimulated by military needs. In America the first such machines were made by the Army Quartermaster's Depot at Fort Holabird, Maryland, which built a number of its own designs in preference to commercially available models which were more expensive and not necessarily exactly suited to army needs. Several different 4×4 designs were made at Fort Holabird, of which the one and a quarter-ton Group 1 Standard Truck was perhaps the most significant as it was a forerunner in conception of the threequarter-ton Dodge which was built in vast numbers during the Second World War. It was powered by a 4.5-litre, six-cylinder, air-cooled Franklin engine, and was made in armoured car versions as well as a general load carrier capable of transporting ten soldiers or a 75 mm field gun. The QMC project lasted only from 1929 to 1932, after which the truck industry brought pressure to bear so that they could supply the Army with their own commercial products.

One of the staff at Fort Holabird was Colonel Arthur W. Herrington who moved to Indianapolis in 1931, and joined forces with Walter C. Marmon to make all-wheel drive vehicles under the name Marmon-Herrington. These were large 6×6 trucks and tractors including those used to operate the Damascus–Baghdad desert bus service. In 1935 Marmon-Herrington made its first 4×4 conversion of a Ford half-ton truck, installing a transfer case and driven front axle under an otherwise standard Ford product. This became a very important part of its business, and the company supplied command cars, trucks, station wagons and ambulances, initially to the Army, but also for civilian purposes. At the same time other manufacturers such as General Motors and Dodge began to get

The British Army tests the Pavesi 8 × 8, c.1932

into the field of the light 4 × 4; GM soon concentrated on heavier trucks but Dodge became the leading supplier of command cars and trucks in the half- to one-ton field during the Second World War.

By the late 1930s, the US Army felt the need for a smaller vehicle than the half-tonners of Dodge and Marmon-Herrington, which could be manhandled out of rough spots and would not need to carry more than a quarter-ton load. In mid-June 1940 they laid down specifications for a four-wheel drive vehicle weighing not more than 1300 pounds. The only company to deliver within the 49-day deadline was American Bantam of Butler, Pennsylvania, a small firm which had made light cars based on the British Austin Seven. The company came up with a simple 4 × 4 four-seater powered by a 45 bhp Continental engine which fitted all the Army's requirements except that it was overweight at 1850 pounds. This was not too much of a drawback, especially since the rival vehicles from Ford and Willys were heavier still, but what Bantam could not do was deliver in the numbers that the Army wanted. Small numbers inevitably meant higher prices, and so the major contracts went to Ford and Willys which eventually built over 600,000 of the vehicle which came to be known as the Jeep. Bantam made a mere 2642 before turning to the manufacture of Jeep trailers.

In Europe Germany was in the forefront of 4 × 4 car development, as one would expect from the great encouragement given to military programmes by the Nazi government from 1933 onwards. One of the most unusual was the Tempo G1200, a light, four-seater command car powered, like the 1905 Christie, by two separate engines, one driving each axle. The engines were 596 cc, two-cylinder ILO units, and the car featured independent suspension all round. It was made from 1936 to 1939, and was sold, mainly for military use, to 40 countries including Sweden, Romania, Argentina and Mexico. Mercedes-Benz made a number of command cars with four-wheel drive and steering, but the standard 4 × 4 of the *Wehrmacht* was designed by the Horch division of Auto Union and made by it and Opel. This had an 80 bhp V-8 engine, all-round independent suspension and some models could be had with four-wheel steering. A variety of open and closed bodies were fitted. Other light medium 4 × 4s were made by Steyr in Austria and Tatra in Czechoslovakia, while the Soviet Union had its own Jeep-type vehicle in the GAZ-67, and also made 4 × 4 versions of its regular GAZ-11 four-door saloon. In Britain 4 × 4 command cars and light trucks were made by Humber, and light trucks by Guy and Morris-Commercial. Heavier 4 × 4 trucks and tractors were made by all the warring nations, and were too numerous to list.

There can be no doubt that without the spur of war the development of four-wheel drive would have been much slower, and without the Jeep who knows if the present vast range of 4 × 4 recreational vehicles would ever have come into existence.

Nick Georgano

WARTIME AUSTERITY,

As the world slowly came to terms with the fact that the Second World War was at last over, tractors which had recently dragged howitzers were turned to clearing the devastation they had wrought. Eisenhower's glowing appraisal of US industry's contribution, that America could not have won the war without the 'Bulldozer, the Jeep and the C-47' could now be seen as a blueprint for the tools needed to gain order for peace. Luckily for those who needed them, a large proportion of the 639,244 Willys MB and Ford GPW quarter-ton utility vehicles – 'Jeeps' – were left in the detritus and even factory fresh in the delivery depots as surplus to requirements. Having crippled its commercial truck building industry after the First World War by selling off war-surplus vehicles on the home market, the US Government had no intention of shipping these vhicles home. Thus it was that civil motorists in Europe and the Far East were to gain their first experience of the benefits of four-wheel drive.

The development of the Jeep has been amply covered elsewhere, but as the first wholly successful, mass produced, lightweight four-wheel drive, it was to provide the basis for most of those which followed. At the end of hostilities as the various Allied powers made the gradual transition to peacetime levels of equipment and manning, the value for those Jeeps which found a way onto the surplus market ran extremely high.

Such was the demand that most governments found it necessary to allocate Jeeps on a priority basis. This ensured that a fair number would find their way into the hands of the farming community and forestry workers. As an interim measure to bridge the gap until tractor production could be restarted, the Jeep did sterling service in many parts of the world. It did have some drawbacks, but at a time when half a loaf was better than none at all, people tended to overlook these and adapt what was available to their needs.

In the main, the drawbacks of the Jeep centred around its limited load carrying capacity and high fuel consumption. To remedy the first, such companies as Duriez in France and Met-a-Met in Great Britain began to turn to making the Jeep more of an all-round proposition. Variants were developed with larger load and flat-bed rear areas, small trucks featuring a forward control cab

Austrian Steyr 4 × 4 field car, 1938

were offered, and at a more rational level, several different weather protection options were marketed. From this experience it was but a short step to fitting the ubiquitous MB with a shooting-brake body to make it an acceptable all-terrain conveyance for the gentleman farmer. It was one such gentleman farmer who was to provide the logical European successor to the Jeep.

Beset by the problems of steel shortage and political mis-direction, the British motor industry was staggering lamely to its feet following the war. For a company such as Rover, which had specialised traditionally in providing the English professional classes with a solidly reliable but unadventurous range of saloon cars, the problem of how to integrate itself into the new, austere socialist Britain proved a headache. Steel was allocated on a basis of a proportion of export trade, and Rover had never been forced to look anywhere but locally for its markets. In fact, in 1945 and 1946 it had no export department whatsoever.

To overcome this problem Maurice Wilkes, a director of Rover and a farmer, suggested that they should build a type of Jeep with an alloy body, because aluminium was not restricted by government quotas, and mainly proprietary Rover components. This would take advantage of the replacement market which was beginning to arise as the more battered war surplus Jeeps ground to a halt. Having used a Jeep himself, Wilkes knew just how to improve upon it without losing the original functional ruggedness. Fuel consumption had to be cut, as many power take-offs as possible had to be incorporated, the panels and fittings had to be easily replaced by the semi-skilled mechanic but, most of all, the new machine had to offer more creature comfort to its operator than the stark military vehicle it replaced.

The vehicle which emerged in 1948 offered all that Wilkes or his contemporaries could have asked of it. Competitors wasted no time in nicknaming it 'Rover's Bastard', but it sold from the moment the world saw it. Incorporating as it did all Wilkes' ideas plus the legendary reliability of the pre-Leyland Rover company, the Land-Rover became the standard off-road vehicle, not only of the British farmer but of almost every major international expedition, and later standard equipment in most of the Third World armed forces.

So successful was it that plans for an overt luxury version of the car, provisionally aimed for launch in the mid-50s, were dropped as the maker struggled unsuccessfully to meet demand. Even so, many private manufacturers seized the chance offered by the long wheelbase Land-Rover Safari to offer luxury long-distance and caravanette conversions.

Meanwhile, Willys Overland had not been slow to realise the potential civilian market for Jeep-type vehicles in the USA. As early as 1946, the CJ2 (for Civilian Jeep) made its appearance, along with the Jeep Model 463 seven-passenger station wagon which featured all-steel bodywork and a reworked drive and suspension package from the MB. Other variations included a panel van and a public utilities vehicle. These vehicles were to help

PEACETIME UTILITY

The Jeepster, a Jeep for post war prosperity

now comes a dream of a car . . . a daring, fun-loving dream,

realized in steel and chrome . . . ready to thrill those "special" kinds of

people of every age who tire of the ordinary and always seek the uncommon:

meet the **Jeepster**

The fleet, low-slung lines of the Jeepster tell you in
advance: "Here is a companion for carefree moments".
Come, sit under the wheel, and deny if you can
the desire to roam new roads with the Jeepster.
Take off from the crowded highway, the mob is
not for you. Seek the unspoiled spots and strange scenes.
Go with the wind, commanding the power of
the mighty 'Jeep' engine. And soon, you'll settle
back in the seat with a smile . . . For this is *fun.*

If you're headed for the shore, the mountains,
or a brisk turn on the boulevard,
your spirits will run high with the Jeepster.
Vacation journey or workaday errand alike are
less tiring, because there's a lift to your spirits.
Leave the more formal cars to more formal people.
You'll drive the Jeepster for the sheer joy of
driving, of going somewhere, with laughter
in your heart and a song on your lips.

Meet the Jeepster now, at Willys-Overland dealers.

MAKERS OF AMERICA'S MOST USEFUL VEHICLES

WILLYS-OVERLAND MOTORS, TOLEDO, OHIO, U.S.A. •

Willys Overland to a profit of some $3.3 million in 1947, the best year for the company since 1928. All the pick-up and utility versions came equipped with a choice of either four- or two-wheel drive. Surprisingly, the majority sold were of the latter variety.

These vehicles were, however, at best fairly agricultural in nature and what was deemed necessary by the management of Willys Overland was a car which combined the practical virtues and the respect that had built up for the MB's capabilities with more sporting appeal. Thus in 1949, to an accompaniment of the kind of advertising superlatives which only the copywriters of an age unfettered by product liability laws could contrive, the Jeepster was announced.

To modern eyes, the Jeepster looks something of a mechanical monster with its Jeep-type grille, cutaway MG TC-type doors, luxury deep-padded front bench seat and pressed steel disc wheels. In fact for those who expected to find the resilience and 'go anywhere' capability of the MB incorporated beneath its ungainly styling, it was to prove a great disappointment. Although the advertising copy offered the freedom of the woods and the deserts for the man who wanted to be rid of the herd, the Jeepster was only available in rear-wheel drive form. Its real impact was not in what it was, but in the thinking which lay behind it: the first rationalisation of the growing movement in the USA to 'get away from it all'.

Perhaps the Jeepster was too far ahead of its time in the way in which it anticipated the markets of the late sixties and the leisure-conscious seventies. In off-road circles it is fashionable to date the start of the four-wheel drive leisure movement to the early sixties and ignore such lightweight four-wheel drive vehicles as the fifties produced. In essence, such a view may well be justified, but it is an extremely narrow one, and one which tends to obscure some of the very worthwhile developments which were to influence the growth of off-road pursuits in the coming years.

In 1943, Toyota had been presented by the Imperial Japanese Army with a number of captured Bantams, and asked to develop a similar car as a replacement for the smaller and underpowered Kurogane 4 × 4 which had been the standard Scout Car of the Japanese forces since the mid-1930s. The result was similar in appearance and far more powerful, having Toyota's own 85 bhp engine. It appeared in the world market in the early fifties, having been seen in Japan as early as 1948, and immediately began to challenge the established market leaders, both in price and its enviable record for reliability. Meanwhile the MB had provided Nissan with inspiration for the Patrol. The Japanese Army was at this time, however, using the M38 produced under licence by Mitsubishi.

These two Japanese vehicles were to be the first trickle of a steady torrent. As the fifties progressed and the Japanese economy grew under shrewd management from an export-orientated government, every major car manufacturer began to look at the success of these two cars and examine the market potential for its own four-wheel drive variants. By the end of the sixties, only Honda and Toyo Kogyo were missing from the line-up of Japanese car manufacturers who had not introduced or were not actively developing four-wheel drive products.

In the USA, under a working brief from Aramco who

Ford GP for the British Army, 1941

were busily opening the oilfields of Saudi Arabia, Studebaker built a prototype four-wheel drive car based on the bodyshell of its 1949 Commander Sedan. Price and complexity rendered this project a non-starter for commercial production, although the principal design was certainly sound, for Bantam had used a great many Studebaker components in their original Jeep prototype.

In France, Delahaye, working under the auspices of the French Army, built a four-wheel drive vehicle, drawing heavily upon the technology gathered from its pre-war luxury tourers. A civilian version, known as the Delta, formed the basis and the military version, known as the VLRD, was accepted by the army as a replacement for the Jeep in 1950. The engine was a four-cylinder in light alloy with dry sump lubrication. All-round independent suspension by torsion bar was featured, and a 24-volt electrical package was added to make it an extremely sophisticated machine.

The driving standards of the French Army were never quite up to the level required to extract the best from this powerful and quick machine, and several fatal accidents arose from the drivers' lack of skill or forgetfulness in taking the vehicle out of four-wheel drive for road use. In 1954 a revised and improved version with the serial number 53 was developed, but by this time Peugeot had developed its 203RA and Delahaye was absorbed by Hotchkiss, which had already reached an agreement with the Kaiser Corporation (which had taken over Willys in 1953) to produce Jeeps in France. In fact a licence to produce Jeeps had been granted by Willys to Hotchkiss in 1952, although serious production did not get underway until October 1956 with the JH102. In the face of competition from Peugeot, the Army decided on the Hotchkiss Jeep as standard equipment and thus ended the career of what could have been the basis of a very luxurious general purpose vehicle.

In 1955, Californian racecar constructor Frank Kurtis was approached by a Saudi prince to build two four-wheel drive Chrysler New Yorkers. This he did, in the process extending the chassis by some seven inches. Other modifications included torsion bar suspension and a revised front chassis to keep the ride height of the car as near to standard as possible. Although extremely beautiful, the cars proved somewhat impractical for serious production due to cost, but served as a marker in the development of the luxury four-wheel drive vehicle.

By the mid-1950s, Alfa Romeo had joined the ranks of the military four-wheel drive builders, as had its traditional Italian rival, Fiat, with its Campagnola. In Great Britain, the Austin company was proving inept at grasping the principle, producing first the Austin Champ, powered by a Rolls-Royce engine, which appeared in 1952, and then in 1957 the Gypsy, a machine which had no redeeming features and one that was an unashamed and extremely inferior copy of the Land-Rover. In Austria, the Steyr-Puch company had produced the simple but brilliant Haflinger, which was to find a ready market among NATO forces, and Mercedes-Benz was developing the Unimog.

Following a tradition of racing-orientated companies, Mercedes had examined the possibility of four-wheel drive when at the peak of racing development in the early fifties, but finding that in endurance racing it would not compensate for the degree of superiority enjoyed by the Jaguar, and that in Formula One it was not needed, the project was abandoned. Thus it was left to a somewhat maverick British engineer named Harry Ferguson to make the definitive moves in the field.

Ferguson had made a niche for himself in the international world of automotive design by originating the power take-off principle for agricultural tractors. When Ford infringed upon his patents he sued, and won at an international level. Having made his point and a vast amount of money, he devoted his remaining years to the problems of four-wheel drive. His aides in this venture were an extremely capable engineer, Tony Rolt, and an ex-racing driver and mechanic, Freddie Dixon, who had started to examine four-wheel drive with a view to making it more competitive in racing cars in the late 1930s.

The first public showing of the Ferguson system was the revolutionary P99 four-wheel drive racing car. It was announced in 1960, the year of Ferguson's death, and unlike the various crude devices from the likes of Bugatti and Alfa Romeo which had graced the world's racing tracks, it proved competitive enough to give Stirling Moss victory in the 1961 Oulton Gold Cup. The FF system, as it became known, replaced the mechanical components used in conventional drive systems of the time, with a set-up which included a viscous coupling to feed torque to the front and rear axles, while alleviating the problems of wind-up which had previously made permanent four-wheel drive impractical. There had of course been more or less successful attempts at four-wheel drive racing cars ever since the Spyker brothers' 1906 victory in the Birmingham Car Club Hill Climb.

In 1946, Porsche was commissioned by Piero Dusio to build a Formula One racecar conforming to the 1.5-litre super-charged Formula of the day, under the name of the Cisitalia. Based around a tubular space frame, and featuring a flat 12-cylinder engine mid-mounted behind the driver, the car drove all wheels through a five-speed, all-syncromesh gearbox. From the cockpit the driver could, by manipulating a lever, also select two-wheel drive when needed for the more open and faster circuits. Here however, Porsche's genius for over-complication tended to prevent the car from ever becoming competitive, for

Dusio ran out of funds and the cars were seen in action only when he had transferred his operation to Buenos Aires. The Cisitalia did once capture the South American flying kilometre record, driven by one Clemar Bucci. The car is now in the Porsche museum.

The success of the P99 brought various other manufacturers of racing cars into contact with the Ferguson system, and it was especially successful in the United States, where Andy Granatelli of STP fame used it to feed four-wheel drive to the wheels of his Novi V-8-engined car. In 1964, Bobby Unser drove the car at Indianapolis but, in a collision with another car, damaged it to the extent that it could not be restarted. The car returned in 1965, but an oil leak caused its retirement that year. In 1966 the car was driven by Greg Weld, but did not complete qualifying.

In 1967, Granatelli tried again, this time with a turbine-engined car powered by a Pratt & Whitney engine, driving through a modified Ferguson system. The car was driven by Parnelli Jones and led the field before retiring with a transmission failure. At this time Colin Chapman joined forces with Andy Granatelli, bringing with him his turbine-powered Lotus 56. Again a Pratt & Whitney engine was used, but this time the Ferguson's centre differential was connected to the output shaft by a morse chain effectively removing the need for troublesome and heavy transfer gears. In all, four of these cars were entered but none finished due to various mishaps, one of them tragic when Mike Spence was killed during practice. During the race, Graham Hill crashed into a wall after losing a wheel, and Art Pollard and Joe Leonard, the other two drivers, were lost with broken fuel pump drives.

For 1968, the Lotus 56s were joined at Indianapolis by the Lola T150 of Al Unser, which featured an all new four-wheel drive system developed by the Hewland Engineering Company in Great Britain. Here, Unser spun out of the race at 40 laps. The following year, 1969, proved the swansong of four-wheel drive cars at Indianapolis when the organisers finally banned their use.

In Formula One, Lotus used a combined ZF and Ferguson system with its 1963 model, powered by a Cosworth DFV engine, while the Matra MS84 used a Cosworth engine, a five-speed Hewland gearbox, and a Ferguson four-wheel drive system. Neither of the cars was particularly successful due to the weight penalty involved in incorporating the four-wheel drive systems. The McLaren M9A again used a Hewland gearbox and a Hewland and ZF limited slip differential. The car, though only ten lb heavier than its two-wheel drive M7A variant, was still unsuccessful, due mainly to the complexity of the four-wheel drive system. As aerofoil technology became more sophisticated and tyres became more efficient, Formula One constructors moved away from four-wheel drive in favour of other ways of finding the grip and downforce which they needed, thus ending the chapter of four-wheel drive in Formula One.

While all this had been taking place significant developments had occurred in the USA. By the mid-fifties Jeep had been persuaded that future prospects for four-wheel drive vehicles would revolve around load-carrying capacities. From this it deduced that a range of forward control vehicles was necessary, and in switching the emphasis of production in this direction, left open a sector of the market which others were quick to isolate and occupy.

Impressed by the success of the long wheelbase Land-Rovers and Land Cruisers, several oil companies were switching traditional suppliers in favour of the British and Japanese machines. This fact, plus the movement in farming circles to these products, impressed the International Harvester Corporation to the extent that it entered the market in 1961 with a light truck with extremely civilised passenger accommodation. Known as the Scout, it was available in two- or four-wheel drive versions, and featured a box section chassis and a 152 cubic inch four-cylinder engine developing 93 bhp. By 1962 the Scout had created a sensation by storming the emergent recreational vehicle market. So successful was it that in 1965 when the range was expanded, International Harvester had deduced that some three-quarters of all production was being bought by non-business users. Within a year, Jeep had hit back with the Wagoneer aimed squarely into this newly roused market, whilst General Motors and Ford immediately added luxury options to their recently introduced FWD pick-ups.

It was to be 1965 before Ford entered the FWD leisure market with the Bronco. Announced for the 1966 model year, the Bronco was an attempt to capture the traditional Jeep market in much the same way that the previous year had seen the introduction of the Mustang in an attempt to capture the potential sports car buyer by offering a reasonably priced package with a high level of equipment. At its introduction, three models were available, the Model 96 Roadster, the Model 97 Pick-up and the Model 98 Wagon. While the Model 97 was expected to compete at basic level with the CJ5 and the basic Scout, the Model 98 was seen as an immediate rival to the Wagoneer and the plusher Scouts.

For 1965, Jeep had finally made some concession to public demand by issuing a special edition of the CJ5, known as the Tuxedo Park. It featured individual front bucket seats, special paint and chrome grille and wheel trims. By this time a list of custom parts available from non-Jeep sources for the CJ series was beginning to point to the superb 'poseur'-type vehicles of the seventies. To match this, Ford offered a breathtaking catalogue of chromed accessories for the Bronco.

1966 saw the formal introduction of the four-wheel drive Supercar. Styled by Vignale and powered by Chrysler, the strikingly handsome Jensen Interceptor made its debut at the Earl's Court Motor Show. Both standard two-wheel drive and FF versions were on show, and both were available to order. Unlike previous Jensen products, which had been built of glass fibre, the sleek body of the Interceptor was built of steel. This aside, the major structural and mechanical components were retained from the Jensen CV8. Thus the car was extremely rigid, due to the ladder-type tubular chassis. Due to the well-proven 6.2-litre engine, the car was also extremely fast, and when all this was coupled to Ferguson's transmission, the result was nothing short of sensational.

Jensen had always maintained an enviable reputation for the ability to build extremely fine examples of the grand touring car. The interiors of each of its products reflected traditional British coachwork at its best. As well as this, the handling of all Jensens had to satisfy the Jensen

Beginnings of the Japanese invasion – 1948 Nissan Patrol

British dead end, the Austin Champ

Thoroughbred sire, the prototype Land Rover

brothers themselves, and in this department too the cars gave nothing away to any exotic competitor. Thus the FF with its typical Ferguson layout with the transfer box to the left of the torque-flight box in front of the central, or master, differential and its torque split of 37 per cent front and 63 per cent rear, was an improvement on a car which was already good and not an attempt to endow a second-rater with acceptable handling.

To many past owners and road testers, the Jensen FF was just the ultimate car. The hypercritical L. J. K. Setright, writing in *Car* in December 1966, spoke of having to approach the car from a completely new viewpoint in order to fully understand the superiority conferred by the Ferguson system. *Motor* magazine, in accordance with its hard driving philosophy, tried first lifting off, and then braking at the apex of sharp high speed bends. It reported little difference in handling besides a slight tendency to tuck in. Only the Dunlop Maxaret brake system attracted criticism due to its imprecise feeling. However this early version of ABS was soon to disappear from the market, as Girling bought the development and production rights from Dunlop for further development.

During its brief but memorable production run nothing but praise was heard, both from the press and from owners. So good was the response that even though it was privately admitted in the factory that the car was uneconomic to build, production was maintained for over four years. The very existence of this super-expensive supercar was enough to help promote the sales of its normally-driven stablemate, and whilst Jensen's profit was assured by building such cars as the Sunbeam Tiger and the last of the great Austin Healeys, the lack of profit on the FF was deemed offset by the public relations benefits.

Just why the Jensen FF was never seen in competition remains something of a mystery. The company standpoint was that the system was never well enough proven to risk on the tracks. The work's development in conjunction with GKN, and known as the FFF, tends to contradict this, insofar as it ever existed.

The FFF was designed as a mobile testbed for the various automotive components originating from GKN. It was powered by a 600 bhp Chrysler Hemi, and once more utilised a Torqueflite box in conjunction with Ferguson four-wheel drive. In the wet the car was capable of a 0–100 mph time of 12.2 seconds, and on a dry road this came down to 11.5 seconds. Bearing in mind that at this time Jim Hall's Chaparral cars were running very competitively with about the same power output and a similar automatic transmission, it would appear that in this form the Jensen FF would have been extremely competitive in long distance racing.

Unfortunately all good things end, and as US Federal Regulations and abysmal mismanagement in the British car industry killed off the last of the true sportscars, so too production economics caught up with the Jensen FF. Faced with a decline in its traditional role as subcontractor to the larger manufacturers and the nearly non-existent profitability of its own progeny, Jensen replaced the FF with the normally-driven SP in 1970, thus ending the production run of the first (and some informed individuals still maintain, the greatest) four-wheel drive supercar.

As the Jensen died in Britain, so Chevrolet in the US joined the major manufacturers involved in the leisure

Detroit muscle, the '62 Jeep Wagoneer

Worldwide workhorse, 1953 Jeep CJ-3B

Glamour Jeep, the '65 CJ-5A Tuxedo Park

market when it introduced the Blazer. In many ways reminiscent of the Bronco, the Blazer was introduced with four-wheel drive as an option. Its good looks and the aggressive marketing campaign began to establish it almost as soon as it appeared, yet it was not until the GMC-badged Jimmy appeared on the scene two years later that the market was well and truly stormed. By this time, yet another important luxury FWD development had made its appearance, one which was to influence off-road luxury for the next ten years by staying well at the forefront of the market.

Luxury Four Wheel Drive

1970 was the year in which luxury four-wheel drive came of age. Not only did International Harvester introduce its all new Scout II which was larger, faster and more stylish, and also carried a full range of engine options from a four-cylinder to a large V-8, but also it marked the emergence of the Range Rover. The Range Rover had its roots in the stillborn project of the early fifties to build an estate-bodied Land-Rover with saloon car comforts, but it was not until the V-8, 3.5-litre light alloy engine was acquired from Buick in 1965 that a viable power plant for such a vehicle was available to the Rover Company. By 1970, Rover had been absorbed into the Leyland Group, and Leyland management saw the Range Rover as a potential flagship for their whole range.

Powered by the superb V-8 engine with styling by Leyland's corporate design department, the car created a sensation on its announcement. Its development had taken only a matter of four years with the first prototype actually running in 1967. Development of the vehicle had been largely in the hands of Peter Wilkes, the nephew of Maurice Wilkes who had first invented the Land-Rover, Spen King and Gordon Bashford. It was their enthusiasm which carried the project through to its successful conclusion against a certain amount of doubt from the more established corporate men at Rover, who felt that the Land-Rover as a utilitarian vehicle fulfilled all the needs which could be asked of it.

Several innovative ideas in off-road technology were to see the light of day in the new vehicle, not the least of them being all-round disc brakes, which in off-road conditions are supremely practical insofar as they dry far quicker than drum brakes and are more easily accessible for maintenance, and long travel coil suspension, which was the first on any vehicle of the kind, for although independent front suspension was available as an option on the Ford Bronco and was standard by this time on the Jeep Wagoneer, fully independent suspension all round as a standard measure was entirely new.

The problems created in a two-door vehicle for off-road use in mounting seatbelts were overcome very neatly by incorporating the seatbelts into the rear of the front seats, thus when the seats tipped forward for access to the rear, the belts disappeared and didn't impede progress. Some criticism over the years has been levelled at the width of these front doors and their weight in opening and closing. However, the reason for adopting a two-door shell with a rear opening hatchback was to maintain rigidity in the original vehicles. A spin-off of this was the delightfully clean styling, which was adopted at an exhibition at the Louvre in Paris as an example of modern sculpture.

Although expensive by the standards of the day, the Range Rover created its own market. Not only did it appeal to those people who needed a practical vehicle for towing horseboxes, for getting round farms or estates, or for simply reaching their holiday cottages or pursuing hobbies such as fishing, but it caught on with the smart set who wanted a practical vehicle with good luggage accommodation, but at the same time the occasional off-road facility. Some lead was given by the British Royal Family, who took to the Range Rover almost as soon as it was announced. Very soon, under pressure of the demand

which had been created for it, good used examples were fetching as much or more than brand new factory produced examples, and by 1973 the waiting list from the factory had increased to some 18 months for the British version.

Almost everyone who came into contact with the Range Rover in its first guise had nothing but praise for it. In 1970 it emerged from the Earl's Court Motor Show with a gold medal for its coachwork. It also won the Don Safety Trophy in the same year, and in 1971 gained the Royal Automobile Club's Dewar Trophy for outstanding technical achievement. The initial marketing campaign for the vehicle stressed its all-round capabilities and emphasised that here was more than one vehicle under the same skin. It was sold as a smart estate car, a practical workhorse and a first-class off-road vehicle. These points were universally corroborated by all contemporary Press tests. In short, the car was everything that everybody at Rover had hoped.

As introduced, its permanent four-wheel drive system featured a third central differential, which was of limited slip type. This was replaced after a year for the company felt that it was over-complicated and that there was no real need for it. Certain other minor changes in production had allowed the output to rise from ten a week when introduced to some hundred a week by the beginning of 1972. This was a mere drop in the ocean when it came to supplying demand, but given the problems of the Leyland Group at the time it represented a very significant production triumph.

Among the first and most loyal customers for the Range Rover were the British police, who realised that with this 100 mph vehicle they could not only keep pace with speeding offenders but be on the scene of motorway accidents with a fair load of equipment very much faster than with the normal truck or van of the type that they had been using until that time. This duality of purpose has served the police well over the years, and as the Range Rover was to develop it was to find an echo in certain other specialist vehicles which were to arise, such as the field ambulances and the stretched airport tenders. However, at its introduction these were but hazy shadows, for the demand for Range Rovers meant that the likelihood of any of them being converted was extremely rare.

Probably the first indication that the Range Rover was going to achieve forms other than those originally intended by the factory came when Carmichael of Worcester, a company with long traditions of building specialist bodies on Land-Rover chassis, built an extended airport tender. This featured a 35-inch extension in the wheelbase and six-wheel drive. The load carrying capacity was also increased and the vehicle made its debut in 1974 to much acclain in international circles. By this time certain upmarket companies specialising in providing transport to the super-rich had started to experiment both with convertible Range Rovers and with extended wheelbase four-door Range Rovers. Chief among these were perhaps Chris Humberstone's Rapport Company which was based in Park Lane, FLM (Panelcraft), and Wood and Pickett. Wood and Pickett had achieved a lot of success in the mid-1960s by providing stylish accoutrements for the then currently fashionable Mini. It was thus but a short step to providing fashionable accoutrements for this latest upmarket vehicle from Leyland. The company provided light guards, crash bars, and superb interiors, not to mention specially commissioned wheels for the car and conversions which would make it totally acceptable to those who were more normally used to driving in a Daimler or a Rolls-Royce. This range of cars was named the 'Sheer Rovers' and continues in production to this day, being extremely successful in such parts of the world as Saudi Arabia, where it is not unusual for a customer to want to spend up to three times the initial purchase price on his Range Rover in order to have it built to his specification.

Another company which has been extremely successful in this market has been Glenfrome of Bristol. Glenfrome is perhaps the only company to have completely rebodied and successfully sold a Range Rover derivative when it introduced its so-called desert sportscar, the Facet, in 1981. Aimed squarely at the 17- to 21-year-old market in the oil-rich Arabian Gulf, the Facet may not appeal to Western eyes, but caused a sensation when it was unveiled in the 1982 Riyadh Motor Show.

Among other companies who have over the years built beautiful conversions on Range Rover chassis, the name Townley Cross-Country Vehicles must be included, for the interesting point of its conversions is that not only is the chassis extended but it is widened at the same time. This is extremely useful for some of their more generously-proportioned rich customers. Like the other aforementioned Range Rover converters, Townley Cross also provides convertible Range Rovers as well as extended six-wheel drive Range Rovers, but in the beginning specialised in building luxury Land-Rovers. It can be truthfully stated that in the specialist companies the workmanship is of a degree almost unknown anywhere else in the world. Such niceties as walnut veneered dashboards, deep pile carpets, cocktail bars, TVs, videos, stacking stereos, climate control and real Connolly leather hide are just some of the options which these specialists provide, making the Range Rover in its various guises an extremely luxurious and at the same time totally practical vehicle.

In the USA the competition in the recreational four-wheel drive movement was reaching new heights. The emergence of the Bronco caused American Motors in 1967 to reintroduce the Jeepster concept of styling and continuing development saw the J100-series Wagoneer and its various derivatives grow into an extremely luxurious and practical off-road transport matching both the General Motors and Ford products for engine and trim options.

General Motors had introduced the 'Suburban' range in the early sixties with a view to capturing the lucrative mining and lumbering fleet market and, in 1967, had brought out the Fleetside version complete with a 327 cubic inch V-8 and an extremely flashy, state-of-the-art luxury interior. In the smaller product ranges the GMC Jimmy, the Chevrolet Blazer (which had been completely redesigned for 1973) and the Ford Bronco were selling strongly with improved power packages into a market which the first three years of the seventies saw expanding at a rate of some 25 per cent per year.

Nor was this increased awareness of the virtues of four-wheel drive confined to the recreational sector for, in the five years between 1966 and 1971, production of

Ford's F100 and F250 series of FWD pick-ups rose from 10,429 to 148,935. Admittedly the false demand created by the Vietnam war impinged upon these figures, yet the trend was to remain remarkably constant in proportional terms throughout the light truck producers in the USA even when military demand dropped.

Taking advantage of this growing market, the third of the US motor giants, Chrysler, launched the last and possibly the definitive dual purpose FWD in 1974, simultaneously announced as the Dodge Ramcharger and with minor trim changes the Plymouth Trail Duster. Chrysler opted for a package which would utilise the best of its well established FWD pick-up components with the expertise gained from building luxury two-wheel drive vans and recreational vehicles.

At its introduction the Ramcharger offered a choice of a 225 cubic inch straight six-cylinder motor, a 318 or 360 cubic inch V-8 or, for those who really felt the need of extra oomph, the fabulous 400 or 440 cubic inch hemi V-8s. The wheelbase was 106 inches which allowed it to compete with the smaller Scouts, the Jimmy and Blazer and the Wagoneer.

In Ramcharger guise, it came in two basic packages – the AD100 which retained two-wheel drive and the AW100 which offered full time FWD utilising Chrysler's New Process version of the Ferguson formula. Although with its overall length of 184.6 inches and its rear overhang of 45.2 inches it was not the most manoeuverable machine, for those who needed the ultimate off-road capability of the Land-Rover or Land Cruiser it acquitted itself extremely well against its US-built opposition in press tests and off-road use generally.

As well as the convenient transmission package with its optional limited slip differential and LoadFlite three-speed automatic, areas of interest included the SE interior and exterior option packages. With its detachable hard top in place and the air conditioning and cruise control in operation, the driver could sit back in the deep padding of the comfortable individual bucket seat and enjoy the Ramcharger as a luxury road car. With the top removed or replaced by the optional soft top and the rear seats removed he had an entirely different vehicle with a genuine half-ton payload and 'get you most places' capability.

Another important and interesting development in the US market of the early seventies came about as the result of an almost inexplicable gap in the commercial market which was spotted and immediately exploited by the ever-vigilant Japanese. As the process of building a pick-up version of medium sized family cars lost ground in Europe, so the Japanese began to move into this sector. Using the floor pans of production cars extended to give full six foot load area length, Toyota produced the Hi-Lux range of pick-ups whilst their great rivals, Nissan, countered with an almost indistinguishable product before almost every other Japanese maker jumped on the band-wagon. So popular were these light trucks that it was a foregone conclusion that they would receive the attention of the customisers who had wrought such startling changes in the basic vehicles from the major US manufacturers.

With demand far outstripping supply, the Hi-Lux found itself a starring role in the post-petrol crisis, dual purpose, light leisure vehicle market. Conversions were marketed allowing enough lift from the standard running gear for the installation of four-wheel drive while the fibre glass experts, who had long ago provided almost every type of US pick-up with an occasional camper facility, soon got busy and produced miniature versions for these far eastern imports.

Never slow to spot a market trend the Japanese soon adapted the current craze for their own purposes. What had started out as a cut price vehicle for the builder, especially aimed at the emergent third world and built tough to survive unmade Middle Eastern and African roads soon started to sprout eye-catching factory paint jobs. Multi-coloured stripes and metallic colours matched with light alloy or stylish pressed steel spoked wheels. Sun dim glass and air conditioning became standard fittings on the top-of-the-range models and four-wheel drive was added as a factory option. In fact so successful was this new bargain-priced means of getting all terrain motoring that both Chevrolet, with its Luv, and Chrysler began importing Japanese models for sale under their own badges.

Unaffected, it seemed, by any vagary in the cost of fuel, Range Rover pursued its single engine policy, but in 1980 announced a four-door factory built variant of the car. This was long overdue but had been held back mainly by the inability of the British Leyland Corporation to fund the extra production needed to cope with the four-door. At the same time, the Series Three Land-Rover with the V-8 engine was announced, although the suspension was still of the old cart-sprung variety that Land-Rovers had been introduced with in 1948. Not until the introduction of the 110 Series Land-Rover in 1982 was the coil suspension of the Range Rover featured in it. This coupled with the County interior and exterior trim finally provided the world with a fairly luxurious Land-Rover.

Meanwhile the impact of the Range Rover on the larger Japanese manufacturers could be seen insofar as both the Nissan Patrol and the Toyota Land Cruiser were re-packaged in the mid-1970s into far more luxurious vehicles. In the case of the long wheelbase Patrols and Land Cruisers, these were treated to facelifts which gave them styling which was equally at home in the middle of the desert or parked outside the local supermarket. These extremely desirable vehicles were to spearhead a new second generation of Japanese four-wheel drives into the world market.

Somewhat atypical of these are those from Suzuki. With the SJ30 series Suzuki opened a market which nobody had realised existed. Using a small 360 cc two-stroke engine, Suzuki produced what must be the world's smallest Jeep-type vehicle. Far from being a gimmick, this proved an absolute boon to the Third World farmer who could afford nothing larger or better, and its small size and light weight gave it the kind of 'go anywhere' characteristic which not only enabled it to capture the cheap fun market but allowed it to work in the most hostile terrain. In its latest guise of the SJ410 Rhino (Jimny 1000 in some markets), the Suzuki represents not only first-class value for money but, where needed, an extremely sophisticated tool for the farmer or forester. It is available with power take-offs, with special capacity tyres and a whole host of specialist equipment which, because of astute

marketing and Japanese production techniques, make it an extremely competitive vehicle in world markets.

By the eighties the Japanese had finally started to show the world the way in the matter of more accessible four-wheel drive for the non-sporting, non-agricultural motorist. As early as 1974 Subaru had added four-wheel drive to its conventionally driven 1600 cc station wagon and promoted the car as a civilised dual purpose vehicle with the added safety of increased traction in dangerous road conditions.

So confident were they in their system that by the time the car was launched in the USA in 1975 they were offering a full guarantee on all major components regardless of use. For the smaller recreational pick-up market they also provided a vehicle named the Brat (an acronym for Bi-drive Recreational Altering Transporter) which was a stylish little pick-up avoiding US federal truck regulations by having two rearward facing plastic seats in the rear load area. Both vehicles were to prove star sellers for Subaru and having established the pattern with them the company went further and added four-wheel drive to all the models available, in the process creating a precedent which still stands for being the only company to do so.

Other companies took an altogether different route. Mitsubishi, who still build Jeeps for the Japanese army, made an effort to provide a really viable off-road vehicle by using their 2.5-litre petrol engine to a 92.5-inch wheelbase giving it five gears with high and low ratios available, adding automatic freewheeling front hubs to obviate wind-up and consequent tyre wear in road use and adding an extremely civilised interior. To further spice the package a turbocharged version is offered with 145 bhp on tap and, for those territories which need diesel engines, a choice of either a 2.3-litre 75 bhp normally aspirated engine or a turbocharged, but ostensibly similar motor, which gives 95 bhp. Sold as the Pajero in some territories and the Shogun in others it represents an interesting package typical of the more traditional approach.

Impressed and influenced by the success of the Range Rover, Isuzu created a perfect miniature version of it. Powered by a 2.2 litre four-cylinder diesel and having a wheelbase of 90.55 inches, the Rodeo, as it is known, is certainly one of the best looking off-roaders and its success in the tough Arab markets points to it being far more than just a pretty face.

1976 Ford Bronco

One of the lessons which these two vehicles amply demonstrate as being well learned by the Japanese is the need to keep styling at a very high level. When General Motors re-packaged the Jimmy and the Blazer in 1973 it was to meet the need of the man who requires something smarter than the purely agricultural and functional and, as the cheaper four-wheel drives from Eastern bloc and newly emergent industrialised countries start to take hold of the bottom end of the market, the importance of style as well as quality must become a governing factor in the mass FWD market place.

Another important factor in the marketing of the new generation of off-road four-wheel drives is the need to find economy without sacrificing the power or the ruggedness which allow off-road vehicles to fulfil their allotted functions. From 1973 General Motors and Ford have pursued a policy of down-sizing their various engine options in favour of six rather than eight cylinders. It is a continuing trend which has seen even Chrysler discontinue its larger engine options and Land-Rover, its small block V-8 notwithstanding, retaining the four-cylinder layout which it had stolidly adhered to despite criticism of obsolescence since the model's inauguration.

Perhaps the most logical and interesting development of the early eighties came about when a series of press ads for American Motors proudly announced, 'The Eagle Has Landed'. The bodyshell, derived from the Hornet-Concorde line, was familiar, the engine and drive train package was both well proven and well known and the combination proved to be the most practical application of the dual purpose FWD family car that the world had yet seen.

For the first time, a full-sized production car was endowed with the equipment to give it the means to leave the road and unlike the smaller, less capacious Subaru range, it was a native US product. Available with either a 2.5-litre 105 bhp four-cylinder or a straight six 4.2-litre 120 bhp engine and a variety of transmission options which allowed either a five-speed manual or three-speed automatic, the Eagle was the first serious attempt to translate the rising acceptance of FWD into an all-round acceptable package for the American public.

Its prime market was to be the 'Snow Belt' territories – those states which suffer deep snow almost continuously from late October until March. Not only was the New Process system useful in navigating snow which drifted across the roads but it also allowed much greater confidence and security when the periodic thaws and refreezing turned the roads of such states as Michigan, Ohio and Indiana into gleaming sheets of ice. Backed as it was with American Motors' reputation in the Jeep market and sold through their excellent dealer network, it met a market need which had hitherto been blissfully ignored by the big four American manufacturers.

Assembled in Canada, the Eagle's success has thoroughly disproved the accusation levelled when it first appeared of being merely a gimmick to extend the production life of the ageing body tooling of its forebears. Even in central Europe the car has claimed a ready following especially in the mountainous regions of Switzerland and Austria where both comparatively low purchase price and extremely reasonable fuel economy have helped it face up to the traditional European competition. As a market pointer, the Eagle must be seen in its own light as one of the most important automotive developments of the era and one of the more pleasant.

The Mystique of the Jeep

As in all other markets fashions tend to come and go in four-wheel drive. As the new generation of smoothly-styled estate cars and mass market saloons with their selectable, front wheel drive or 4×4 make themselves the dual purpose market leaders, so the demise of the heavier if more powerful American vehicles has become more and more apparent. As the Land-Rover and its immediate competitors have become ever more sophisticated (and expensive) so the lighter, more economic products of the Third World will begin to bite in sectors where once there was no vehicle choice at all. The one major exception to the rule lies with the machine which started the ball well and truly rolling, the Jeep.

Perhaps somewhere, some day, a Jeep freak with a flair for statistics will work out the total production of the traditional style Jeep. It would certainly be a complex task for he would have to take into account all the licence-built products from as far afield as France, Japan, China, Kenya and the 'pirated' versions made or remade in the back street workshops of such countries as the Philippines. Obviously some qualification would have to be made, for instance whether or not to include the 'Jeepsters', but with or without these the total would be phenomenal.

From the practical standpoint, the appeal which has led to this long and plentiful production life is obvious, the Jeep is amazingly robust and extremely reliable with parts readily available almost anywhere. Yet this in itself cannot explain the way that, year after year, more and more people who have little need of these attributes buy Jeeps. The allure lies just as much in the timeless aesthetically pleasing but supremely practical styling which has changed little since the Jeep made its debut in 1941. Like those other long-lived trendsetters the VW Beetle and the Citroën 2CV the Jeep made no concession to current styling practice at its conception and remains above it to this day.

The Jeep has always had the ability to inspire friendship and loyalty amongst its devotees. This can be seen as readily when two or three Golden Eagle or Laredo owners meet outside a fashionable Chelsea pub as at the annual gathering of the gallic faithful who pit their machines against appalling terrain in the heart of French Basque mountain country in the Rallye Des Cimes. Admittedly, to those oblivious to the charms of the Jeep, these people could be dismissed as adults emulating on the road the enjoyment they derived from their childhood toys.

The cult of the Jeep probably resides highest in Northern California's Great Divide in the little unspoilt frontier township of Georgetown. There in 1950 one Mark Smith and some friends got together to provide a challenge for all the local Jeep drivers over the old and nearly impassable Rubicon Trail while, at the same time, ensuring that it would be fun.

The first 'Jamboree' to be run over the old wagon trail was in 1953 after thousands of feet of timber had been manhandled to the halfway point of the trail to provide the first dance floor and the comfort of ready built toilets. Some 55 Jeeps and 156 people took part that year and so successful was this concept of part party and part mountain rally that the numbers soon took off. These days some 400 vehicles including a few Toyota and California resident Land-Rovers take part.

To find out why the Jeep rules supreme on both the Jamboree and the Rallye Des Cimes it is necessary to go back to basics and look at the vehicle in detail. The fact that usually it is the older Jeeps which claim the honours gives an important clue, for the success of the Jeep lies not only in its toughness, but the lower gear ratios carefully chosen to meet the conditions of war. These gear ratios plus the short wheelbase and minimal front and rear overhang allow the Jeep to get in and out of the worst and the tightest terrain the organisers can find for it. So efficient is the Jeep in really rough mountain country that the organisers had to ban almost all other four-wheel drive vehicles due to the time it took to tow them out of trouble. Nobody, after all, likes to be held up on the way to the Jeepers' party with its gourmet food and plentiful champagne all brought in by helicopter.

Another compelling reason for the popularity of the Jeep must reside in the build quality. Basic it may be, but badly put together it has never been. The same can be truthfully said of its stablemate the Grand Wagoneer which still appears remarkably similar to its first public appearance in 1963 and steadily sells as its rivals downgrade size in the name of economy. In terms of size, Jeep makers American Motors are far more akin to a medium-sized European manufacturer than the US big three. Unlike them they cannot afford costly retooling each year to sort out the whims and vagaries of the car buying public. They sell on quality and in this the reputation of the ubiquitous Jeep needs no further commendation.

The Performance Generation

If the Audi Quattro had performed less spectacularly either on the sales floor or on the international rally circuit it would be easy to dismiss it as one of the motor industry's more expensive flights of fancy. In fact the Quattro has gained that rare distinction of taking a competent, if unexciting, manufacturer of middle class medium price saloons into the same class as Mercedes, BMW and Volvo. It has also spawned a whole new breed of 'homologation specials' which tread very closely upon the hallowed ground of the immortals such as Porsche and Ferrari in terms of performance while staying nearer in price to the basic bread and butter machines which shaped them. In short the Quattro has been a phenomenal marketing success.

The story of the Quattro begins with two unrelated events in 1975. The first was the surprise win of an AMC Jeep on the 'Press On Regardless Rally' (North America's only round of the International Rally Championship) and the second was the unveiling by VW-Audi of its new engine range. Reaction to the Jeeps' win was slow but sure, especially when it showed itself to be competitive on more than one club event in Canada. The major European teams lobbied and successfully obtained from the authorities a ban on four-wheel drive on the rally front.

Soon the good showings were being passed off as a fluke and the Jeep was conveniently forgotten.

Faced with an increasingly competitive middle market sector and finding that its four- and five-cylinder engines lent themselves well to the careful tuning of the international experts, Audi and VW took to the racetracks with the Golf GTi and the 80. Good showings were made by drivers of the calibre of Richard Lloyd and Stirling Moss and the interest generated on the tracks started to show in the sales figures. The next logical step was to confront direct market rivals on the rally tracks where that rare but precious animal 'the man in the street' could see a car which looked remarkably like his own fighting through the world's most appalling terrain against one which looked remarkably like his next door neighbour's.

Here luck deserted Audi for the standard 80 was just not up to the kind of competition provided by long term exponents of the field such as Ford, Saab and Lancia. Occasional class wins in second line events were not what the board of Audi had had in mind and for some time it began to look as if the factory would quit the rally-go-round in favour of some less demanding means of product promotion. At this point, competitions manager Walter Tresor began to add the rest of the ingredients to what he considered was a potentially viable up-market road car with competition potential.

In response to the German Army's new generation light vehicle requirement, VW-Audi (VAG) had produced a vehicle named the Iltis as a replacement for its long-lived Munga model. In reaching the standards of reliability and sophistication demanded by the army, they had evolved a lightweight but reliable and robust transmission package which of necessity had been mated to the current range of four- and five-cylinder engines. Here it should be noted that with true German pragmatism the four- and five-cylinder engines shared many components and the five was in fact almost entirely a four with another cylinder tagged on the end. The Iltis reached the German Army in 1976 and at about the same time the board of Audi sanctioned the offering of a turbocharged version of the top of the market 2.2-litre five-cylinder 100 range of saloons.

By adding the four-wheel drive system to the Audi 100 Turbo coupé, Tresor was seeking to give his company and his competition department the edge on its rivals. Before this could come about, however, certain members of the VAG hierarchy had to be convinced of the potential of the project. This Tresor realised was a major obstacle. In most car companies it can take years for an idea to gain currency and then it is usually changed beyond recognition by the technical staff. By first building the car and then demonstrating its validity at the very top, he realised, he might just get his project through. Taking an 80, he built the prototype he wanted and, having obtained a cautious agreement from the board to fund further development, he took it first to Hockenheim where it performed well against normally driven rivals and then issued an invitation to the then head of VAG, Toni Schmucker, to test drive the car.

Tresor's test drive has gone into the annals of motoring folklore for he simply hired a fire engine, soaked a hillside and invited Schmucker to attempt it in any of the corporation's normally driven products. While Schmucker and entourage could hardly get beyond the starting point in the normally driven cars, all were capable of conducting the FWD 30 up the steep and slippery surface. From the cautious go ahead given in September 1977 to full board approval took only a matter of some six months and in February 1980 the rest of the world took its first look at the new wonder car on the Audi stand at the Geneva Autoshow. Only the FIA remained to be convinced that the Quattro was a serious proposition and to this end Audi began to lobby to have the FWD ban lifted from international rally events.

Keeping the products of America's fourth largest manufacturer from international rallying may have been quite straightforward for the Paris based administration of the FIA, after all there was only one American delegate on the international motorsport committee, but banning VAG with the attendant bad press it would have created was another matter entirely. By enlisting the support of Gerard Larrouse at Renault and Cesare Fiorio at Lancia the competitions department at Ingolstadt managed to get the ban lifted and celebrated in fine style when, as a proving exercise, Hannu Mikkola and Arne Hertz pulverised the opposition in the Algarve Rally in October 1980. Fortunately for the opposition's wounded pride the car was not an official entry and therefore claimed no points, but the writing had gone onto the wall and the portents for 1981 looked heavily weighted in Audi's favour.

The official debut of the Quattro was on 9 January 1981 and two days later Austrian Franz Wittman made it a first time out win for the car as he collected the laurels for his native country's Castrol Janner rally. By this time it was rumoured that the rally car was giving some 420 bhp against the road car's 200. It was also rumoured that the factory were having problems with turbo lag and with handling on the over-run. Within a short space of time the factory was admitting that the rumours were true. Works drivers Mikkola and Frenchwoman Michele Mouton along with their regular partners Arne Hertz and Fabrizia Pons were having to learn a whole new technique of driving and as if this was not enough the service crews had never served in the front line of international rallying before. The early promise was fading fast and the rival teams were beginning to heave sighs of relief.

The official works team debut was on the 1981 Monte Carlo rally. It was a debacle of the first order as Mouton retired with fuel contamination and Mikkola crashed out whilst holding a six-minute lead. Things could only improve. With the Swedish Rally in February they did with Mikkola exploiting the icy conditions perfectly to bring the car home to a resounding first international victory. The pattern repeated itself when the bulk of the rally was away from the tarmac, with the result that the Quattro carried off the 1982 Manufacturers' championship. No mean feat when Lancia had jumped the gun by exploiting the regulations to the maximum and introducing the first genuine Group B (as opposed to the less powerful and heavier Group 4 machinery) rally car in the form of the Monte Carlo based 037.

By 1983 Walter Tresor had left the fold, instead of promoting Quattros within the company he had chosen to build his own shop specialising in super tuning road going Quattros. With Lancia running away with the Manufacturers Championship, the competitions department desperately sought to remedy the Quattro's tarmac handling shortcomings to the extent that at one point they brought the long time Renault and Citroën exponent Bernard Darniche into the company to try and sort the suspension. All was in vain. The company's salvation was due to come from the Group B evolutionary car, the Quattro Sport. With its shorter wheelbase, more accessible major component layout and lighter weight, the 'shortcut' is the last card left in the deck for the supercar from Ingolstadt. Already the 200 homologation cars have become collectors pieces.

Already there is talk of a further evolutionary engine for the Quattro Sport with four valves per cylinder liberating in excess of 500 bhp. Further improvements in handling can be expected from the revolutionary new electric clutch fitted to these cars which allows left footed braking without sacrificing the standard all synchro box for a crash box. In effect this overcomes the turbo lag without the need for the radically expensive solutions to this problem encountered elsewhere in competition, notably Formula One racing.

On the sales front, the Quattro created problems due to its very success. Not only is it an exclusive car but its very high level of sophistication ensures that it will always remain so in its ultimate road going form. For this reason it became almost an embarrassment to Audi who measure their performance in production figures of 2000 to 3000 units per day. For a company so geared to build what is in effect a supercar, whole segments of the production process had to be rethought. The Quattro as the flag carrier of the Audi range had to match the products of Porsche, Mercedes and Jaguar for quality of construction. Its complexity thus demanded that it be largely hand built. To do this a whole new precision assembly line was installed at the Ingolstadt factory. Men with a work cycle acclimatisation of perhaps two minutes had to be retrained to accept cycles in excess of 16 minutes and to be able to do every job in their particular production sector. Thus the 20 or so Quattros which leave the line each day can truly claim to be craftsman built, at the same time the company gained a microcosmic study area for new production techniques.

With the success of the Quattro and the onset of the Group B regulations, informed opinion began to speculate upon the probability of further FWD developments in the competition field. With the opening of the 1983 model season the speculation was confirmed as international manufacturers began to unveil future plans.

From France came the news that Citroën were preparing a 4 × 4 variant of their delightful little 1434 cc Visa rally car. Known as the Mille Pistes after the rally in which Citroën have traditionally performed well, the 200 examples needed for homologation were prepared and ready for sale amost as soon as the official homologation was granted on 1 March 1983. Although very much a product of Citroën's newly revitalised competition policy, the car was actually developed by Denis Mathiot, an outside contractor, under the direction of Citroën's Guy Verrier.

In essence the creation of the Mille Pistes has been kept remarkably simple with the drive to the rear limited slip differential being taken directly from the crownwheel of

The performance generation arrives. The Lancia Delta Turbo 4 × 4 however remained a prototype only

the front. To alleviate lock-up or wind-up problems Citroën have incorporated a torque limiting system in the rear drive train. To further reduce strain on the transmission an uncoupling device controlled by a button on the dashboard and utilising vacuum power has been added to allow easy manoeuverability in tight situations. The only residual weak point in the system is that the front limited slip differential now has to take the torque loading for all four wheels. Although not an outright contender for overall honours the car comes into its own where nimbleness and light weight are at a premium. Events, in fact, such as the Milles Pistes.

Another interesting development from France is the Peugeot 205 Turbo 16. Designed by development engineer Bernard Perron, the car mixes a remarkable amount of state-of-the-art rally technology to provide a unique machine. Power is provided by a development of the road going 205 GTi's XU series engine which has been uprated and turbocharged to give some 320 bhp. To provide the weight distribution Perron desired, 555 kg front and 655 kg rear, the engine has been mid-mounted and turned through 90 degrees whilst the two 55-litre glass reinforced plastic fuel tanks have been tucked beneath the front seats.

To transmit the power to the wheels, a derivative of the five-speed Citroën SM gearbox has been used driving through a Ferguson viscous coupling. Overall weight distribution has been further optimised by locating the

radiator well forward and positioning the air/air intercooler for the KKK turbocharger to the left of the engine where it is fed by an air intake incorporated in the rear wing moulding. The talents of Renault Formula One turbocharging expert Jean-Pierre Boudy, who had been attracted to the project, ensured that the lag which so characterised the early Audi Quattro has been largely overcome. The resulting car is an out and out rally machine, regardless of the fact that road going versions are selling well at some £25,000 each and promises long term serious competition for the rally establishment.

Although the reputation of Porsche has traditionally resided on the racetracks of the world it came as no surprise to the cognoscenti when the Stuttgart company unveiled their Group B challenger at the 1983 Frankfurt Autoshow. As announced, the car made an interesting conversation piece equipped as it was with a drive system incorporating both Quattro components and those of Porsches' own design. Optimum torque split in this smoothly styled 911-based vehicle was to be achieved by the use of sophisticated electronic sensors feeding information back to activate a three- or five-plate clutch housed in its own oil bath, the amount of slip on this clutch would thus determine the torque feed to the wheels minimising the effect of irrational components such as the driver.

At the time of writing little more has been seen of this Group B car but, early in 1984, another and possibly even more interesting four-wheel drive 911 variant arrived from Zuffenhausen and promptly won the gruelling Paris–Dakar off-road rally. In effect the device which Porsche produced incorporated a fairly standard 3.2-litre turbocharged engine driving a Quattro transmission, modified by the incorporation of an epicyclic gear system to achieve a torque split of 70 per cent at the rear to 30 per cent at the front. The front axle was a modified Porsche 924 transaxle and power was taken to it by the drive shaft from the 944. The bottom was protected by a ten millimetre thick pan formed from carbon fibre and double wishbones were used instead of the standard front suspension. The car was designed and produced in only three months and as well as providing Ren Metge and Dominique Lemoyne with the overall win it handed Jacky Ickx sixth place on his first attempt in the event.

Yet another interesting four-wheel drive production car derivative for Group B is the MG Metro 6R4. This car was developed by Williams Grand Prix Engineering at the request of Leyland Competitions, and features an all new V-6 engine which in fact is three-quarters of the well-proven 3.5-litre, V-8 Rover unit powering the Range Rover, turbocharged and feeding four-wheel drive through a proprietary Ferguson transfer box. In initial testing the car proved extremely competitive, with only some 310 bhp on tap. Should it be seen in competition, however, this could easily be increased. It points the way to future co-operation as well between the Austin Rover group and Honda, who has traditionally specialised in four-valve V-6s, for example its championship-winning Formula Two engines.

For its international rally contender the Mitsubishi corporation took the prime car from its middle range. Its four-wheel drive Group B machine is based firmly on the Starion Turbo, and can at least claim to be one of the most standard-looking of all of these cars. However, in order to make it a competitive proposition, Mitsubishi has enlisted the help of Alan Wilkinson, whose pedigree includes development experience with the Ford Competitions Department, Toyota Team Europe and Audi Sports UK. Although the chassis is shortened from that of the normal Starion, a lot of proprietary Colt parts are retained. For instance, transfer boxes from the four-wheel drive Pajero-Shogun, with the internals modified to cope with the extra power.

So pronounced is the drift toward four-wheel drive in rallying circles that even Lancia have been influenced. Informed speculation suggests that the replacement for the all-conquering 037 series will be a Delta look-alike using the floor plan and mechanicals from the 037 and incorporating a Haoland manufactured FWD transmission system.

The Current Crop

Perhaps the ultimate acknowledgement of the importance of the growing four-wheel drive market was the emergence in the late seventies of the Mercedes-Benz Gelandewagen, better known as the 'G-wagen' or, as Mercedes themselves prefer, the G Series. Although in fairness it should be admitted that as it was primarily designed as a military vehicle, the presence of the three pointed star on the G Series has led to a spate of unfavourable comparisons

between it and the Range Rover. In fact the G Series is far more suited to comparison with the 90 and 110 Series Land-Rovers or the Toyota Land Cruiser and Nissan Patrol.

Available in open and hard top versions with long (112.2 inch, 2.85 m) or short (94.49 inch, 2.4 m) wheelbases, the G Series offers a choice of power plants comprising 2.3- and 2.8-litre petrol engines and 2.4 or 3-litre diesels. As introduced, the cars certainly betray their original military orientation for they feature neither independent suspension nor climate control. The development of the vehicles was actually carried out by Steyr-Daimler-Puch in Austria and as such they can claim to be the direct lineal descendents of the superbly successful little Haflingers which still command a staunch following in off-road circles both in Great Britain and on the continent.

Perhaps the most interesting feature of these vehicles lies in the transmission for they were the first available with individually lockable differentials, a boon in deep mud or soft sandy conditions. As regards interior trim, the up-market options certainly offer more luxury than any of the direct competition and even in the diesel variants interior noise levels are commendably low while both the rigidity of construction and detail finish give nothing away to any other vehicle in their class. As with other Mercedes products the main objection to the machine is the price, for, in a market which is noted for the longevity and reliability of all the front runners, these traditional Mercedes virtues tend to be taken for granted. Even so the G Series has made some inroads to the international market and the next few years should decide whether it can be developed to a point where it becomes a serious rival to the Range Rover.

Further down the price scale, Portugal has entered the market with both a version of the Romanian designed ARO, known as the Portaro, and an updated derivative of the French designed Cournil known as the UMM. In its top of the range 'Argocat' incarnation (as sold in Britain) the UMM offers the type of no frills value for money which the series one and two Land-Rovers and Land Cruisers built their reputations upon. Powered by a 2.5-litre Peugeot diesel, the Argocat is far nearer in concept to a pick-up or light truck than a dual purpose vehicle but offers surprisingly comfortable accommodation for the driver and passengers over extremely rough terrain. The Portaro offers both utility and station wagon variants both powered by the Daihatsu 2.5-litre four-cylinder diesel. The top of the range 260 Celta Turbo offers a useful 95 bhp at 4000 rpm with air conditioning and a sliding roof available to order. Again the market aim is to take advantage of the rising costs of the traditional Land-Rovers and their Japanese equivalents.

The Dangel company in eastern France manufactures an interesting and extremely rugged four-wheel drive conversion for the Peugeot 504 pick-up known as the Afrique utilising the standard Peugeot 2.5-litre diesel engine. Also available from the same stable is the four-wheel drive 504 Estate with a choice of diesel or petrol motivation utilising the same transmission system in which four-wheel drive is automatically engaged when low ratio is selected. This vehicle provides an interesting comparison to Renault's 4×4 18 Break which is ostensibly aimed at a similar market.

From Japan Subaru continues to market its line of civilised and attractive vehicles including a delightful 1600 cc hatchback coupé. This free revving little high-performer has been introduced as a sporty alternative 'with a touch of braggadocio for guys and gals on the go-go-go'. This whiskery American advertising jargon certainly does not detract from its off-road performance for the short wheelbase and superb traction make it a practical proposition over all but the most impassable terrain. Its hatchback configuration and compact dimensions also fit it uniquely for the man who needs weekend off-road sporting capacity yet who baulks at the cost of a smart full size off-road vehicle which is a liability to park in inner city areas.

Edging into this market are the Italian manufacturers with Alfa Romeo firmly at the forefront with the 33 4 × 4 Estate. In this instance both development and installation are the responsibility of Pininfarina who has produced a practical and elegant variant upon the original at little cost in economy or tractability. The few criticisms levelled at the car tend to concern the increased noise levels and amounts of body roll in normal road going use. Although well-grounded, these type of side effects are almost unavoidable in this type of conversion and have in the past been levelled at both the Renault 18 Break and the 4 × 4 Toyota Tercel estate car. Meanwhile Alfa's arch rivals Fiat have followed the Mercedes-Benz route to Steyr-Daimler-Puch for the four-wheel drive package on their cheerful little Panda 4 × 4.

Audi has committed itself to a programme which allows a four-wheel drive option à la Quattro on all of its models opening the possibility of a turbo diesel 100 Avant at the top of the range. Meanwhile Volkswagen has added the four-wheel drive Passat Tetra to its product range and announced that the Series Two Golf will be available with four-wheel drive from November 1984 as an M option costing approximately the same as a set of snow tyres. BMW, meanwhile, has adopted a ZF development of the FF viscous coupling set-up for their 3 series 4 × 4s allowing a 40/60 front to rear torque split.

With its long history of building Jeeps under licence, France is the source for European distribution of the more luxurious Jeep variants which are now assembled and marketed by Renault. In order to bring them up to European standards of economy and performance, a brand new 2.5-litre diesel engine is available in the up-market Laredo and Renegade CJ7s.

In the USA, following the introduction in 1982–83 of more compact-sized GMC Jimmys, Chevrolet Blazers and Ford Broncos, 1984 has seen the introduction of a compact size range of Jeep XJ series recreational vehicles in the Cherokee and the Wagoneer. Again American Motors has opted for a 2.5-litre diesel engine as a means of cutting down on running costs, and a new 2.8-litre, V-6 engine has been standardised for the forthcoming European versions of these cars. As well as smaller engines and a smaller body profile, much trouble has been taken to remove weight from the previous models, and a saving of around 1000 lb has been achieved. Both the Cherokee and Wagoneer sport wagons share the same mechanical components, but have distinctive styling which extends to grille treatments, tail lamps, exterior trim and mouldings, as well as interior design, fabric and trim. They are 21 inches shorter, six inches narrower and four inches lower than the former Cherokee and Wagoneer, but they still retain up to 90 per cent of the previous models' interior space. The mechanical components feature a full length ladder chassis welded to the bottom of the frame, similar to both the Land-Rover and the Mercedes G Series. They also, of course, feature Jeep's Quadra-Trak four-wheel drive system, which gives them permanent four-wheel drive when needed, but two-wheel drive is available as an option with both automatic and five-speed manual transmissions.

This choice of transmissions is also a feature of the 1984 Range Rovers, with both two- and four-door versions being offered with either a four- or five-speed manual box, or a three-speed automatic transmission. Previously the only automatic Range Rovers were those available from Schuler with a modified Torqueflite box with an FF set-up which made the already costly Range Rover extremely expensive.

The crop of 1984 models from Japan is almost too varied to list. As well as the superb Rodeo from Isuzu and the 2.5-litre petrol Colt, which has since been joined by a diesel stablemate, Daihatsu have introduced a completely new, updated, restyled and re-engined range of its delightful smaller four-wheel drive models. These, marketed under the name Fourtrak, represent superb fun and practical value for money. Their Achilles' heel would perhaps lie in the smallness of the engine at 1400 cc in its normal form, and their lack of carrying capacity for anything more than a small, normal family. However, as dual purpose city/country vehicles, especially the open versions, they are not only attractive to the eye and easy on the pocket, but have already proved themselves to have the legendary Daihatsu reliability. This will be an interesting company to watch over the next two to three years, for not only has it produced these cars but it has a fine small three-cylinder diesel turbocharged coupé, which again would probably lend itself to four-wheel drive and dual purpose applications.

For 1984, the Nissan Patrol range carries on largely unchanged from its early eighties restyling. New grilles are featured, and new interior options. Neither Nissan nor Toyota need to constantly update what is essentially an extremely good product with a very high rate of customer loyalty in all world territories.

Suzuki's new range of SJ410s features luxury equipment and options which change from country to country and territory to territory. Once again, customer loyalty is such that demand far exceeds supply. Despite the restrictions now in force in Great Britain on Japanese products, a quick telephone call to the local Suzuki agent will find that there is over a year's waiting list on certain models. This points to the emergence of an off-road recreational vehicle market in Great Britain and Europe which, although it has been a long time coming, could in fact mirror that of the States in its impact on automotive sales across the board.

Four-wheel drive then, in its civil applications has come a long way from being something for the farmer, the vet or the *rus in urbe* rich. In the range of vehicles being manufactured today, from high-riding mud wallowers to high-performance road cars, it is one of the most significant automotive trends of the 1980s.

REFERENCE SECTION

ALFA ROMEO ALFA 33 1.5

Although perhaps not living up to the expectations of Alfa purists, the standard Alfa 33 was the car that played the main role in steering the company back to prosperity in 1984. The Alfa 33 4 × 4, with the conversion engineered by Pininfarina, was a natural progression in Alfa's campaign to maintain a presence in this exclusive market.

MANUFACTURER:	Alfa Romeo SpA, Milan, Italy

CONFIGURATION: 4 × 4, front-engined, saloon car

	doors	seats	unladen weight	max load
Alfa 33	5	5	840 kg (1852 lb)	475 kg (1047 lb)

ENGINE:	4-cylinder, 1490 cc, water-cooled petrol developing 85 hp at 5800 rpm
	Torque 121 Nm at 3500 rpm
	Compression ratio 9:1

TRANSMISSION:	Manual, selectable 4 × 2 or 4 × 4
	Type of clutch single dry plate
	Number of gear ratios 5 forward, 1 reverse
	1) 3.75:1 2) 2.05:1 3) 1.378:1 4) 1.027:1
	5) 0.825:1 Rev. 3.09:1
	Final drive 3.55:1

CHASSIS AND SUSPENSION	Unitary construction, independent front suspension by McPherson struts, with coil springs, rigid rear axle, coil springs and telescopic shock absorbers
	Fuel tank 53 litres (11.65 gallons)
	Brakes front discs, drums rear with power assist
	Steering rack and pinion
	Tyres 170/70 SR 13
	Electrical system 12V

DIMENSIONS:	Length 4.015 m (13 ft 2 in)
	Width 1.61 m (5 ft 3 in)
	Height 1.205 m (3 ft 11 in)
	Wheelbase 2.455 m (8 ft)
	Track 1.39 m/1.36 m (rear)
	(4 ft 7 in/4 ft 5 in)
	Turning radius 5.2 m (17 ft)
	Ground clearance 0.15 m (6 in)

PERFORMANCE:	Max speed 170 km/h (106 mph)
	Power-to-weight ratio 9.9 kg/hp (21.82 lb/hp)
	Fuel consumption 7–11 litres/100 km
	(1.53–2.41 gallons/62 miles)

The Alfa 33 4 × 4 was engineered by Pininfarina and launched at the 1983 Frankfurt motor show giving Alfa a toehold in the dual purpose and upmarket 'snowbelt' market. Four wheel drive can be engaged at any speed and the vehicle has higher ground clearance than the standard with a beefed up suspension. In 1984 Alfa launched the Giardinetta estate (inset), like the saloon, featuring a very high level of equipment

AMC EAGLE

AMC Eagle Wagon

Launched in 1980, the Eagle was pitched at a market for a road car but with the traction and road holding advantages of full time four-wheel drive. It has been taken up meanwhile by outdoorsmen as well as city slickers and has a unique slot in the domestic US line-up.

The Eagle is now offered in four-door sedan and four-door wagon variants with a six-cylinder 4.2 litre petrol engine as standard, with selectable four- or two-wheel drive. Transmissions on offer are four- or five-speed manual and three-speed automatic. Trim packages include 'Sport' and 'Limited', a luxury option on the Eagle Wagon.

MANUFACTURER: American Motors Corporation, Detroit, Michigan, USA

CONFIGURATION: 4 × 4, front-engined, saloon car and estate

	doors	seats	unladen weight
Sedan	4/5	5/6	1487 kg (3278 lb)
Station wagon	5	5	1500 kg (3307 lb)

ENGINE:
i) 4-cylinder, 2460 cc, water-cooled petrol developing 105 bhp at 5000 rpm
Torque   175 Nm at 3000 rpm
Compression ratio   9.2:1
ii) V-6, 4228 cc, water-cooled petrol developing 12 hp at 3600 rpm
Torque   284 Nm at 1800 rpm
Compression ratio   8.3:1

TRANSMISSION: Manual, 4- or 5-speed box, automatic, selectable 4 × 2 or 4 × 4

Type of clutch   single dry plate
Number of gear ratios   i) 4-speed box,
                         4 forward, 1 reverse
1) 4.03:1 2) 2.37:1 3) 1.5:1 4) 1:1 Rev. 3.76:1
                         ii) 5-speed box,
                         5 forward, 1 reverse
1) 4.03:1 2) 2.37:1 3) 1.5:1 4) 1:1 5) 0.86:1
Rev. 3.76:1

CHASSIS AND SUSPENSION: Unitary body. Independent front suspension by coil springs, rear rigid axle with semi-elliptical leaf springs and hydraulic shock absorbers

Fuel tank	80 litres (17.59 gallons)
Brakes	discs front, drums rear with power assist
Steering	recirculating ball with power assist
Tyres	195/75 R15
Electrical system	12V

DIMENSIONS:

Length	4.59 m (15 ft 1 in)/ 4.65 m (15 ft 3 in) (station wagon)
Width	1.83 m (6 ft)
Height	1.38 m (4 ft 6 in)
Wheelbase	2.775 m (9 ft 1 in)
Track	1.51 m/1.46 m (rear) (4 ft 11 in/4 ft 9 in)
Turning radius	5.8 m (19 ft)
Ground clearance	0.2 m (8 in)

PERFORMANCE:

Max speed (2.5-litre engine)	140 km/h (87 mph)
Power-to-weight ratio	13.6 kg/hp (29.98 lb/hp)
Fuel consumption	12–17 litres/100 km (2.63–3.73 gallons/62 miles)
Max speed (V6 4.2-litre engine)	175 km/h (109 mph)
Power-to-weight ratio	12.9 kg/hp (28.43 lb/hp)
Fuel consumption	13–22 litres/100 km (2.85–4.83 gallons/62 miles)

ARO 10

The ARO 10, marketed in Britain as the Dacia Duster

The Romanian ARO 10 is sold as the Dacia Duster in certain markets and offers contemporary styling plus a well appointed interior with the kind of rugged engineering ARO have been building into their four-wheel drive vehicles for years. The ARO 10/Dacia Duster is available as a pick-up, a full length hard top, a top of the range station wagon and 'roadster' with open body, tilt frame and roll bar.

ENGINE:
i) Renault 4-cylinder, 1289 cc, water-cooled petrol developing 54 hp at 5250 rpm
Torque   88 Nm at 3000 rpm
Compression ratio   8.5:1
ii) Renault 4-cylinder, 1297 cc, water-cooled petrol developing 62 hp at 5500 rpm
Torque   100 Nm at 3300 rpm
Compression ratio   9.5:1

TRANSMISSION:
Manual, selectable 4 × 2 or 4 × 4
Type of clutch   single dry plate
Number of gear ratios   4 forward, 1 reverse
1) 4.376:1   2) 2.455:1   3) 1.514:1   4) 1:1
Rev. 3.66:1
Final drive   4.571:1
Transfer box   2-speed
              i) 1.076:1   ii) 2.2494:1

CHASSIS AND SUSPENSION:
Ladder frame. Independent front suspension with coil springs and telescopic shock absorbers. Rear rigid axle with semi-elliptical leaf springs and telescopic shock absorbers

Fuel tank   90 litres (19.79 gallons)
Brakes   discs front, drums rear
Steering   worm and roller
Tyres   175 SR × 14
Electrical system   12V

MANUFACTURER: Intreprinderea Mecanica Muscel, Cimpulung, Romania

CONFIGURATION: 4 × 4, front-engined, open body with canvas top, hard top

	doors	seats	unladen weight	max load
10.0	2	2	1120 kg (2469 lb)	410 kg (904 lb)
10.1	2	5	1130 kg (2491 lb)	530 kg (1168 lb)
10.3	2	2	1160 kg (2557 lb)	470 kg (1036 lb)
10.4	2	5	1180 kg (2601 lb)	450 kg (992 lb)

DIMENSIONS:
Length   3.83 m (12 ft 7 in)
Width   1.6 m (5 ft 3 in)
Height   1.65 m (5 ft 5 in)
Wheelbase   2.4 m (7 ft 10 in)
Track   1.3 m (4 ft 3 in)
Turning radius   5.7 m (19 ft)
Ground clearance   0.19 m (7 in)

PERFORMANCE:
Max speed   115 km/h (71 mph)
Fuel consumption   12.5 litres/100 km (2.74 gallons/62 miles)

ARO 240 SERIES

ARO 244 station wagon

The state motor factory, Uzina Mecanica Muscel at Cimplulung Romania began licence production of the Soviet GAZ-69 (see p. 64) in 1964 and continued manufacture for ten years. A new vehicle began to supplant the UMM M461 from 1970 onwards marketed as the ARO and the range was exported from 1972 onwards.

The ARO 240 is a canvas top pick-up, the ARO 243 has a hard top for the cab with a canvas covered load area or conformal steel top and the ARO 244 has four-door station wagon bodywork. Optional equipment includes bench seats running lengthways at rear, a Peugeot-manufactured diesel engine and freewheel hubs.

MANUFACTURER:	Intreprinderea Mecanica Muscel, Cimpulung, Romania				

CONFIGURATION:		doors	seats	unladen weight	max load
	240	2	6	1500 kg (2431 lb)	700 kg (317 lb)
	243	3	6	1620 kg (2486 lb)	700 kg (317 lb)
	244	5	5	1660 kg (2504 lb)	540 kg (245 lb)

ENGINE:	ARO L25 4-cylinder, 2495 cc water-cooled petrol developing 83 hp at 4800 rpm

TRANSMISSION:	Manual	
	Type of clutch	single dry plate
	Number of gear ratios	4 forward, 1 reverse
	Transfer box	2-speed

CHASSIS AND SUSPENSION:	Channel section ladder type chassis. Front wheels independently sprung via coil springs. Rigid rear axle with semi-elliptical leaf springs. Telescopic shock absorbers all round	
	Fuel tank	95 litres (21.34 gallons)
	Brakes	drum brakes all round, hydraulic, mechanical parking
	Steering	worm and roller
	Tyres	6.50 × 16
	Electrical system	12V

DIMENSIONS:	Length	4.035 m (13 ft 3 in)
	Width	1.775 m (5 ft 10 in)
	Height	1.88–2.015 m (6 ft 2 in–6 ft 7 in)
	Wheelbase	2.35 m (7 ft 8 in)
	Track	1.445 m/1.467 m (4 ft 9 in/4 ft 10 in)
	Turning radius	6 m (20 ft)
	Ground clearance	0.22 m (9 in)
	Fording	0.6 m (2 ft)
	Gradient	60%

PERFORMANCE:	Max speed	115 km/h (65 mph)
	Power-to-weight ratio	18.7 kg/hp (41.23 lb/hp)
	Fuel consumption	12–20 litres/100 km (2.64–4.4 gallons/62 miles)

ENGINE:	Peugeot XD 490 diesel, 2.1-litre developing 59 hp at 4500 rpm	
	Max speed	110 km/h (68 mph)
	Power-to-weight ratio	22.9 kg/hp (50.48 lb/hp)
	Fuel consumption	8–14 litres/100 km (1.76–3.08 gallons/62 miles)
	Peugeot 3.1 diesel developing 65 hp at 3200 rpm	

ATW CHICO

ATW Chico shows its agricultural abilities

The Chico was developed by the aircraft manufacturers, Messerschmitt Bolkow Blohm and built by ATW Auto-Monatan Werke with licence production in the Republic of Ireland. It features a three point articulating chassis (the prototype has only two articulating sections) and has been demonstrated with a wide variety of equipment for everything from snow clearing to viticulture in precipitate Moselle vineyards.

MANUFACTURER:	Auto Montan Werke, Frankfurt, West Germany			
CONFIGURATION:	4 ×4, rear-engined, articulated body, open load area with canvas cover, enclosed cab			
		doors	seats	unladen weight	max load
	Chico	2	2	1500 kg (3307 lb)	100 kg (220 lb)

ENGINE:	Deutz 2-cylinder, 1648 cc, air-cooled diesel developing 35 hp at 3000 rpm

TRANSMISSION:	Manual with differential lock	
	Type of clutch	hydraulic, single dry plate
	Number of gear ratios	4 forward, 1 reverse
	Transfer box	2-speed

CHASSIS AND SUSPENSION:	Fuel tank	55 litres (12.09 gallons)
	Tyres	205 R ×16
	Electrical system	12V

DIMENSIONS:	Length	4.09 m (13 ft 5 in)
	Width	1.72 m (5 ft 8 in)
	Height	2.05 m (6 ft 9 in)
	Wheelbase	2.519 m (8 ft 3 in)
	Track	1.5 m (4 ft 11 in)
	Turning radius	10 m (33 ft)
	Ground clearance	0.4 m (1 ft 4 in)
	Fording	0.62 m (2 ft)
	Gradient	60%
	Slew angle around centreline	30°

AUTO-UNION MUNGA

Auto-Union Munga 6

The West German motor industry, rebuilt from postwar ruins, began to develop prototype military vehicles once again around 1954, initially based on simple all-wheel drive derivatives of commercial trucks. When the Bundeswehr was formed in 1956 a large requirement was generated for purpose designed tactical vehicles, where possible within NATO standardisation constraints.

For the quarter-tonne class (cross-country payload rating), 4 × 4 light vehicle requirement, three manufacturers submitted prototypes, Porsche (the Porsche 597 with a rear-mounted, 1582 cc, air-cooled engine in a unitary body), Goliath (with a two-stroke, 887 cc, fuel injection engine) and Auto Union which produced the winning design.

Both Porsche and Goliath models were built in limited numbers for field trials and some reached civilian hands. The Auto Union 'Munga' was standardised and about 55,000 were produced between 1958 and 1968 for both civil and military use. The Munga (Mehrzweck Universal Gelandewagen mit Allradantrieb – multi-purpose universal field car with all-wheel drive) served and still serves with the armed forces of West Germany, Indonesia and the Netherlands and has been used by British and French garrison forces in West Berlin.

In military service there are variants such as anti-tank vehicles armed with Cobra wire-guided anti-tank missiles, radio vehicles and ambulances.

The Munga's chassis is a box section frame with double side members, an all-steel body with removable side doors and folding windscreen plus a canvas top that can be rolled right back. The vehicle is permanent 4 × 4 drive although the earliest 1955–56 models had selectable 4 × 2. There are three basic models: the Munga 4 is a four-seater with seats for driver and three passengers, or up to 375 kg (827 lb) of cargo and towing capacity on roads up to 500 kg (1102 lb); the Munga 6 has bench seats down

each side with a rear tailgate and can accommodate six men or 690 kg (1521 lb) of cargo and haul a braked trailer up to 750 kg (1653 lb) on roads. The Munga 8 has a built up rear section with a three-man bench seat on either side or it can carry 690 kg (1521 lb) of cargo.

MANUFACTURER:	Auto-Union, Ingolstadt, West Germany (1958–1968)			
CONFIGURATION:	4 × 4, front-engined open body with canvas top			
		doors	seats	unladen weight	max load

	doors	seats	unladen weight	max load
Munga 4	—	4	1245 kg (2745 lb)	375 kg (827 lb)
Munga 6	—	6	1425 kg (3142 lb)	375 kg (827 lb)
Munga 8	—	8		

ENGINE:	DKW 3-cylinder, 980 cc petrol developing 44 hp at 4250 rpm

TRANSMISSION:	Manual (early models had selectable 4 × 4 or 4 × 2)	
	Type of clutch	single dry plate
	Number of gear ratios	4 forward, 1 reverse
	Transfer box	2-speed

CHASSIS AND SUSPENSION:	Box section frame with double side members. Transverse leaf springs all round with double-acting telescopic shock absorbers	
	Fuel tank	45 litres (9.89 gallons)
	Brakes	drums all round
	Steering	rack and pinion
	Tyres	6.00 × 16
	Electrical system	24V

DIMENSIONS:	Munga 4	
	Length	3.45 m (11 ft 4 in)
	Width	1.7 m (5 ft 7 in)
	Height	1.75 m (5 ft 9 in)
	Wheelbase	2 m (6 ft 7 in)
	Track	1.206 m (3 ft 11 in)
	Turning radius	6.25 m (20 ft 6 in)
	Ground clearance	0.24 m (9 in)
	Fording	0.5 m (1 ft 8 in)
	Gradient	60%
	Angle of approach/departure	43°/41°

AUDI 80 QUATTRO

Although the factory hand built a 'Quattro' (based on the Audi 80) in 1978 as a proving exercise, the first the world saw of the Quattro concept was with the advent of the 100 coupé version at the 1980 Geneva Motor Show. Its success in world rally championships, and its ready acceptance by those who would normally buy such exotica as the S-class Mercedes Benz, has assured not only the Quattro a place in automotive history, but Audi a place in the upper middle market slot.

With the 80 Quattro, Audi sought to do what AMC managed in the much larger US market with the Eagle within the confines of Europe. The 80 is an attainable performance saloon whereas the Quattro remains a supercar.

Audi are committed to introducing at least one 4 × 4 derivative which will be named 'Quattro' across their whole continuing model range.

MANUFACTURER: Audi AG, Ingolstadt, West Germany

CONFIGURATION: 4 × 4, front-engined, saloon car

doors	seats	unladen weight	max load
4	5	1190 kg (2624 lb)	360 kg (794 lb)

ENGINE:
i) 5-cylinder, 2144 cc water-cooled petrol with fuel injection developing 136 hp at 5900 rpm
Torque 176 Nm at 4500 rpm
Compression ratio 9.3:1
ii) 5-cylinder, 1994 cc water-cooled petrol with fuel injection developing 115 hp at 5400 rpm
Torque 165 Nm at 3200 rpm
Compression ratio 10:1

TRANSMISSION:
Manual permanent 4 × 4
Type of clutch single dry plate
Number of gear ratios 5 forward, 1 reverse
1) 3.6:1 2) 2.125:1 3) 1.456:1 4) 1.071:1
5) 0.829:1 Rev. 3.5:1
Final drive 4.111:1

CHASSIS AND SUSPENSION:
Unitary construction with forward sub frame.
Independent suspension all round by coil springs with telescopic shock absorbers.

Fuel tank 70 litres (15.4 gallons)
Brakes discs all round with servo
Steering rack and pinion with power assist
Tyres 175/70 HR 14
Electrical system 12V

DIMENSIONS:
Length 4.385 m (14 ft 5 in)
Width 1.68 m (5 ft 6 in)
Height 1.375 m (4 ft 6 in)
Wheelbase 2.525 m (8 ft 4 in)
Track 1.405 m (4 ft 7 in)
Turning radius 5.25 m (17 ft 3 in)
Ground clearance 0.12 m (5 in)

PERFORMANCE:
i) 2.1 litre
Max speed 193 km/h (120 mph)
Power-to-weight ratio 8.8 kg/hp (19.4 lb/hp)
Fuel consumption 7.3–13.6 litres/100 km (1.6–3 gallons/62 miles)

ii) 2 litre
Max speed 184 km/h (114 mph)
Power-to-weight ratio 10.1 kg/hp (22.27 lb/hp)
Fuel consumption 7.1–13.5 litres/100 km (1.56–2.97 gallons/62 miles)

AUDI QUATTRO, QUATTRO SPORT

MANUFACTURER: Audi AG, Ingolstadt, West Germany

CONFIGURATION: 4 × 4, front-engined, high performance saloon

	doors	seats	unladen weight	max load
Quattro	2	5	1300 kg (2866 lb)	460 kg (882 lb)
Quattro Sport	2	2 + 2	1000 kg (2205 lb)	

ENGINE:
i) Quattro: 5-cylinder, 2144 cc, water-cooled petrol with fuel injection and turbocharging developing 200 hp at 5500 rpm
Torque 285 Nm at 3500 rpm
Compression ratio 7:1
ii) Quattro Sport: 5-cylinder, 2133 cc water-cooled petrol with fuel injection and turbocharging, four valves per cylinder developing 300 hp at 6500 rpm
Torque 330 Nm at 4500 rpm
Compression ratio 8.3:1

TRANSMISSION:
Manual, permanent 4 × 4
Type of clutch single dry plate
Number of gear ratios 5 forward, 1 reverse
i) Quattro 1) 3.6:1 2) 2.125:1 3) 1.458:1 4) 1.071:1 5) 0.778:1 Rev. 3.5:1
Final drive 3.889:1
ii) Quattro Sport 1) 3.5:1 2) 2.083:1 3) 1.368:1 4) 0.962:1 5) 0.759:1 Rev. 3.455:1
Final drive 3.875:1

CHASSIS AND SUSPENSION:
Unitary construction with forward sub frame.
Independent suspension all round by coil springs with telescopic shock absorbers

Fuel tank 90 litres (19.8 gallons)
Brakes discs all round with servo
Steering rack and pinion with power assist
Tyres 205/60 VR15
Electrical system 12V

DIMENSIONS:

	Quattro	Quattro Sport
Length	4.405 m (14 ft 5 in)	4.165 m (13 ft 8 in)
Width	1.725 m (5 ft 8 in)	1.805 m (5 ft 11 in)
Height	1.345 m (4 ft 5 in)	1.345 m (4 ft 5 in)
Wheelbase	2.525 m (8 ft 4 in)	2.205 m (7 ft 3 in)
Track	1.42/1.45 m (rear) (4 ft 8 in/4 ft 9 in)	
Turning radius	5.565 m (18 ft 3 in)	
Ground clearance	0.17 m (7 in)	

PERFORMANCE:
(Quattro)
Max speed 222 km/h (137 mph)
Power-to-weight ratio 6.5 kg/hp (14.3 lb/hp)
Fuel consumption 7.7–15.4 litres/100 km (1.7–3.4 gallons/62 miles)

Quattro Sport
Max speed 250 km/h (155 mph)
Power-to-weight ratio 3.3 kg/hp (7.3 lb/hp)

Main picture: Audi Quattro, a true craftsman-built, four wheel drive supercar. Inset: Audi Quattro Sport, the 'shortcut' aimed at Group B rally regulations launched with a flourish in 1983

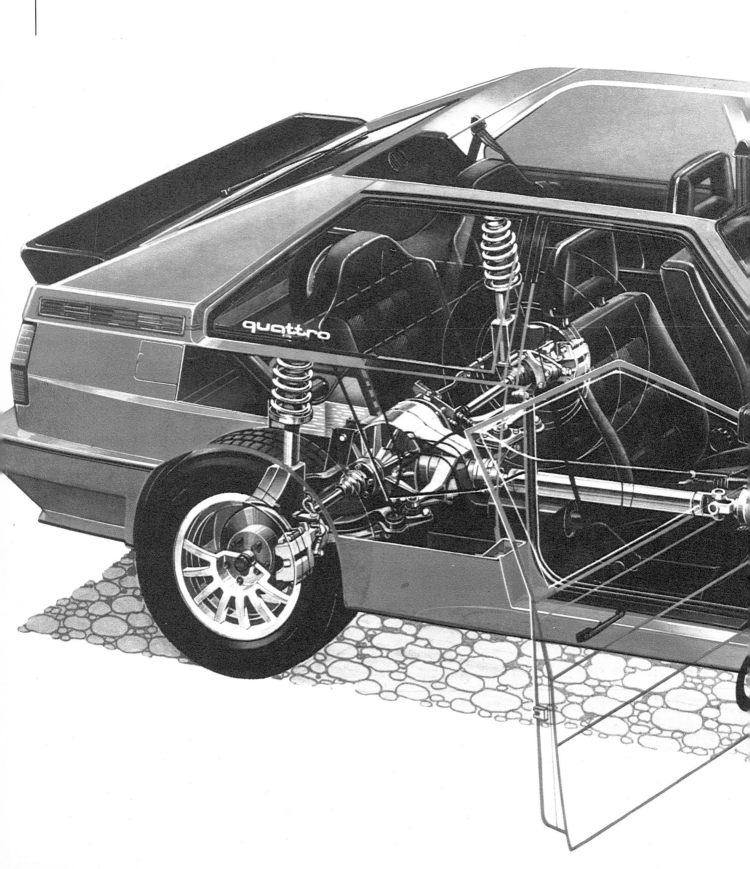

BEIJING BJ-212

BJ 212

A conventional vehicle largely derived from Soviet prototypes and in particular from the UAZ-469B, the BJ-212 serves in large numbers with the People's Liberation Army and also with the army of Tchad. With four doors in a standard jeep-type body with a separate chassis frame, the vehicle has a canvas top and a folding windscreen. The BJ-212A is a two door pick-up with tailgate.

TRANSMISSION:	Manual, freewheeling front hubs	
	Type of clutch	single dry plate
	Number of gear ratios	3 forward, 1 reverse
	Transfer box	2-speed

CHASSIS AND SUSPENSION:	Separate ladder frame chassis. Semi-elliptical springs and hydraulic shock absorbers	
	Fuel tank	60 litres (13.2 gallons)
	Brakes	hydraulic, drum on all wheels, mechanical parking
	Tyres	6.50 × 16
	Electrical system	12V

MANUFACTURER: Bei-Ching Shih, People's Republic of China

CONFIGURATION: 4 × 4, front-engined, open body with canvas top and pick-up, folding screen

	doors	seats	unladen weight	max load
BJ-212	4	5	1530 kg (3373 lb)	425 kg (937 lb)
BJ-212A	2	8	1520 kg (3360 lb)	600 kg (1140 lb)

ENGINE: Model 492, 4-cylinder, 2445 cc, petrol developing 75 hp at 3500 rpm

DIMENSIONS:	Length	3.86 m (12 ft 8 in)
	Width	1.75 m (5 ft 9 in)
	Height	1.87 m (6 ft 2 in)
	Wheelbase	2.3 m (7 ft 6 in)
	Track	1.44 m (4 ft 8 in)
	Turning radius	6 m (20 ft)
	Ground clearance	0.22 m (9 in)
	Fording	0.5 m (1 ft 8 in)
	Gradient	58%

PERFORMANCE:	Max speed	98 km/h (61 mph)
	Fuel consumption	13 litres/100 km

BRAVIA COMMANDO Mk II

One of the many M38A1 derivatives manufactured around the world, the Comando is built in Portugal under license from the Jeep Corporation. It is used by the Portugese armed forces for a variety of military roles and can be mounted with a recoilless rifle with a special divided windscreen to accommodate the barrel.

MANUFACTURER:	Bravia, Lisbon, Portugal			
CONFIGURATION:	4 × 4, front-engined, open body with canvas top			
	doors	seats	unladen weight	max load
	2	1 + 1 + 4	1096 kg (2416 lb)	600 kg (1323 lb)
ENGINE:	i) Model 104 HC, 4-cylinder, water-cooled petrol developing 91 hp at 5000 rpm			
	ii) Perkins 4.154 4-cylinder diesel developing 70 hp at 3600 rpm			
TRANSMISSION:	Manual			
	Type of clutch	single dry plate		
	Number of gear ratios	4 forward, 1 reverse		
	Transfer box	2-speed		
CHASSIS AND SUSPENSION:	Ladder type chassis frame. Semi-elliptical leaf springs front and rear with hydraulic telescopic shock absorbers			
	Fuel tank	40 litres (8.79 gallons)		
	Brakes	drums all round		
	Steering	worm and sector		
	Tyres	6.00 × 16		
	Electrical system	12V		
DIMENSIONS:	Length	3.44 m (11 ft 3 in)		
	Width	1.699 m (5 ft 7 in)		
	Height	1.733 m (5 ft 8 in)		
	Wheelbase	2.057 m (6 ft 9 in)		
	Track	1.234 m/1.232 m (rear) (4 ft/4 ft)		
	Ground clearance	0.204 m (8 in)		

Chevy S/10 Pick-up

CHEVY BLAZER

Chevrolet introduced the Blazer in April 1969 as their answer to the Jeep Wagoneers, the Ford Bronco and the International Scout which had been setting the pace in civil four-wheel drive all through the 1960s. The first Blazer was very straightforward, built on a heavy steel frame with leaf springs all round and an open body with either soft top or removable fibreglass hard top. The Blazer was paralleled by the GMC Jimmy launched in October 1969, identical in everything except radiator grille treatment, badging and trim details, and sold through GMC's truck marketing operation. Both vehicles were refined through the seventies, retaining their boxy, purposeful styling and chromey glamour with a strong appeal to customers who continued to want a big machine around them through the years of Detroit's fuel-conscious restraint. Today the Chevrolet four-wheel drive truck and off road line up includes the S-10 Fleetside 4WD pick-up, the S-10 4WD pick-up with crew cab, the S-10 Blazer 4WD pick-up with tailgate, the K-10 Fleetside and Step-side 4WD long wheelbase pick-up, the K30 Fleetside

4WD with eight foot bed length, the full-size K10 Blazer and the K20 Suburban crew bus/recreational vehicle. The pick-ups are available as chassis cabs and the whole range is offered with diesel engine options. In 1982 Chevrolet launched the down-sized Blazer T-series, paralleled again by a 'Jimmy T.' Max unladen weight is 1895 kg and wheelbase is shorter than the Blazer K. The Blazer T is available with a 2 litre petrol engine, a 2.8 litre V6 petrol or a 2.2 litre Isuzu diesel. A four or five speed manual or three speed automatic transmission is optional.

MANUFACTURER:	Chevrolet Division, General Motors Corporation			
CONFIGURATION:	4 × 4, front-engined, station wagon, hard top			
		doors	seats	unladen weight
	K10/15 Blazer	3	5	2075 kg
ENGINE:	i) 5-litre, water-cooled petrol developing 160 hp at 4400 rpm			
	ii) 6.2-litre, water-cooled V8 diesel developing 130 hp at 3600 rpm			
TRANSMISSION:	Manual or automatic			
	Type of clutch	single dry plate		
	Number of gear ratios	4 forward, 1 reverse (manual) 4 speed with overdrive (automatic)		
CHASSIS AND SUSPENSION:	Box section ladder type with steel body, semi-elliptical leaf springs all round with hydraulic shock absorbers			
	Fuel tank	25–27 gallons		
	Brakes	discs front, drums rear with servo		
	Steering	recirculating ball		
	Tyres	P195/75 R15		
	Electrical system	12V		
DIMENSIONS:	Length	4.71 m (15 ft 5 in)		
	Width	2.02 m (6 ft 7 in)		
	Height	1.875 m (6 ft 0½ in)		
	Wheelbase	2.705 m (8 ft 10 in)		
	Track	1.68 m/1.60 m (rear) (5 ft 6 in/5 ft 3 in)		
	Turning radius	13.1 m (43 ft)		
	Ground clearance	0.18 m (8 in)		
PERFORMANCE:	Max speed	160 km/h (100 mph)		
	Power-to-weight ratio	12.8 kg/hp (27 lb/hp)		
	Fuel consumption	15–24 litres/100 km (3.33–5.28 gallons/62 miles)		

Chevy Blazer T

CITROËN FAF

The Portuguese-built Citroën FAF

Aimed at the Third World market as a utility vehicle, the Citroën FAF comes from the 2CV Dyane lineage with the great majority of the automotive components shared in common. Although it has a leisure market sale, the Citroën FAF has been readily adapted to military use with cargo carrier, command/radio and air-portable variants in service with the French Army while the basic vehicle also serves with the Burundi Army and is produced in Greece as the NAMCO Pony.

Two models are currently in production, a 4 × 4 and a 4 × 2 version, both with 400 kg (882 lb) payloads. A model is also available with a two-place bench seat behind the driver/passenger seats, folding forward to increase the cargo area.

ENGINE:	2-cylinder, 602 cc, air-cooled petrol developing 29 hp at 5750 rpm	
	Torque	33 Nm at 3500 rpm
	Compression ratio	8.5:1

TRANSMISSION:	Manual	
	Type of clutch	single dry plate
	Number of gear ratios	4 forward, 1 reverse
	1) 6.06:1 2) 3.125:1	3) 1.923:1 4) 1.421:1
	Rev. 6.06:1	
	Final drive	3.85:1
	Transfer box	2-speed 2.6:1, 1:1

CHASSIS AND SUSPENSION: SUSPENSION:	Unitary construction with longerons. Independent front suspension, swinging leading arms, telescopic shock absorbers, independent rear suspension by swinging trailing arms linked to front suspension	
	Fuel tank	32 litres (7.03 gallons)
	Brakes	discs all round
	Steering	rack and pinion
	Tyres	135–380
	Electrical system	12V/24V

DIMENSIONS:	Length	3.58 m (11 ft 9 in)
	Width	1.56 m (5 ft 1 in)
	Height	1.586 m (5 ft 2 in)
	Wheelbase	2.4 m (7 ft 10 in)
	Track	1.26 m (4 ft 2 in)
	Turning radius	5.7 m (19 ft)
	Ground clearance	0.18 m/0.24 m (7 in/9 in)
	Fording	0.35 m (1 ft 2 in)
	Gradient	50%

MANUFACTURER: Citroën, Beira Alto, Portugal

CONFIGURATION: 4 × 4, front-engined, station wagon, open body with canvas top

	doors	seats	unladen weight	max load
Station wagon	3	5	840 kg (1852 lb)	400 kg (882 lb)

PERFORMANCE:	Max speed	100 km/h (62 mph)
	Power-to-weight ratio	23 kg/hp (50.7 lb/hp)
	Fuel consumption	7.3 litres/100 km (1.6 gallons/62 miles)

CITROËN VISA MILLES PISTES

The rally-proven Citroën Visa Milles Pistes

The Milles Pistes (named for a rally in which Citroën has had consistent success) is probably the cheapest performance 4 × 4 available. Its simple but robust system offers a partial off-road facility in a class of vehicle which otherwise would be confined to the routine of tarmac. The drive system was developed by Denis Mathiot.

MANUFACTURER:	Automobiles Citroën, Neuilly-sur-Seine, France			
CONFIGURATION:	4 × 4, front-engined, saloon			
		doors	seats	unladen weight
	Visa	5	4	850 kg (1874 lb)
ENGINE:	3-cylinder, 1361 cc, water-cooled petrol developing 112 hp at 6800 rpm			
	Torque		131 Nm at 4500 rpm	
	Compression ratio		10.1:1	
TRANSMISSION:	Manual, permanent 4 × 4			
	Type of clutch		single dry plate	
	Number of gear ratios		5 forward, 1 reverse	
	1) 3.88:1 2) 2.29:1 3) 1.5:1 4) 1.12:1 5) 0.9:1			
	Rev. 3.56:1			
	Final drive		4.067:1	
CHASSIS AND SUSPENSION:	Fuel tank		55 litres (12.1 gallons)	
	Brakes		discs all round with servo	
	Steering		rack and pinion	
	Tyres		190/55 HR 340	
	Electrical system		12V	
DIMENSIONS:	Length		3.69 m (12 ft 1 in)	
	Width		1.54 m (5 ft 1 in)	
	Height		1.41 m (4 ft 7 in)	
	Wheelbase		2.435 m (8 ft)	
	Track		1.33 m/1.32 m (rear)	
			(4 ft 4 in/4 ft 4 in)	
	Turning radius		4.95 m (16 ft)	
PERFORMANCE:	Max speed		185 km/h (115 mph)	
	Power-to-weight ratio		7.6 kg/hp (16.75 lb/hp)	
	Fuel consumption		9–16 litres/100 km	
			(1.98–3.52 gallons/62 miles)	

CITROËN MEHARI ARMEE

Citroën Mehari Armee, military version of a popular recreational vehicle

An open utility body version of the already utilitarian 2CV6 was put into production by Citroën in 1968 and quickly found a leisure market as well as military customers. A 4 × 2 version has been in production ever since with a plastic self-coloured body and some 8000 were delivered to the French armed forces and gendarmerie and to the Spanish Army.

The basic vehicle with an engine of only 602 cc has been adapted as an ambulance and communications vehicle and has been passed in air dropping trials. A 4 × 4 version of the Citroën Mehari was manufactured from 1979–1982 with a two-speed reduction transfer box and disc brakes all round.

MANUFACTURER:	Automobiles Citroën, Neuilly-sur-Seine, France		
CONFIGURATION:	4 × 4 front-engined, open body with canvas hood		
	doors seats	unladen weight	max load
Mehari	– 1 + 1	570 kg	385 kg
Armee		(1256 lb)	(849 lb)
ENGINE:	Citroën AK 2, 2-cylinder, 602 cc developing 29 hp at 5500 rpm		
TRANSMISSION:	Manual		
	Type of clutch	single dry plate	
	Number of gear ratios	4 forward, 1 reverse	
	Transfer box	2-speed	
CHASSIS AND SUSPENSION:	Unitary plastic body with subframes based on chassis of Dyane 6 car. Coil springs and hydraulic shock absorbers front and rear		
	Fuel tank	25 litres (5.5 gallons)	
	Brakes	hydraulic drums	
	Steering	rack and bar	
	Tyres	135 × 380	
	Electrical system	12V (24V optional)	
DIMENSIONS:	Length	3.52 m (11 ft 6 in)	
	Width	1.53 m (5 ft)	
	Height	1.635 m (5 ft 5 in)	
	Wheelbase	2.37 m (7 ft 9 in)	
	Turning radius	5.35 m (17 ft 6 in)	
	Gradient	40%	
PERFORMANCE:	Max speed	100 km/h (62 mph)	
	Operating range	300 km (186 miles)	

CROCO

The Croco is one of the rare breed of articulating off road vehicles

Aimed at the developing Third World utility market and at military customers, the CROCO (Cross-Country) 500 kg (1102 lb) light vehicle is amphibious and is one of the rare breed of 'wasp waisted' vehicles, its body constructed in two separate units articulating around a single central pivot. The vehicle is driven by its road wheels in water or by an optional three-bladed propeller at the rear, driven by a power take-off.

The body units are made of tubular steel with sheet steel cladding and are sealed for flotation in water. The vehicle is designed for the easiest possible maintenance and engine, transmission, electrics or complete body units can be changed in the field in under two hours.

The front unit contains the CROCO-built Wankel-type single-rotor, rotary engine, offset to the right, plus driver and passenger seats. The windscreen folds flat and the canvas top folds back on to the roll bar. All wheels, plus mudguards, steer, and an outboard motor can be fitted for increased operability in water.

MANUFACTURER:	CROCO Ltd., Holziken, Switzerland			
CONFIGURATION:	4 × 4, front-engined, open platform with articulating body			
		doors	**seats**	**unladen weight**	**max load**
	Croco	–	2	900 kg (1984 lb)	500 kg (1102 lb)
ENGINE:	Wankel-type single-rotor developing 32 bhp at 5500 rpm			
TRANSMISSION:	Manual, belt drive			
	Number of gear ratios	2 forward, 1 reverse		
	Fuel tank	83 litres (18.25 gallons)		
	Brakes	discs front, drums rear		
	Steering	rack and pinion		
	Tyres	31.00 × 15.50		
	Electrical system	12V		
DIMENSIONS:	Length	2.7m (8 ft 10 in)		
	Width	2 m (6 ft 7 in)		
	Height	1.95 m (6 ft 5 in)		
	Wheelbase	1.62 m (5 ft 4 in)		
	Track	1.65 m (5 ft 5 in)		
	Turning radius	4.6 m (15 ft)		
	Ground clearance	0.28 m (11 in)		
	Fording	amphibious		
	Gradient	100%		
PERFORMANCE:	Max speed	60 km/h (37 mph) (water via propeller 8 km/h) (4.9 mph)		

DAIHATSU FOURTRAK

The F-80 series 'Fourtrak' was launched in 1983/4

Variously sold as the 'Taft', 'Fourtrak' and 'Wildcat', Daihatsu's attractive range of lightweight off-road vehicles were restyled in 1984 to bring them in line with current dual purpose market demands. They remain serious off-road machines and, in spite of the cart sprung formula, the long action suspension gives them a civilised ride. The F80/F70 series supplanted the F-20 in 1983. Daihatsu also manufactures the tiny Mira saloon car in four-wheel drive form.

ENGINE:	i) Type 3Y 4-cylinder, 1998 cc, water-cooled petrol developing 87 bhp at 4600 rpm ii) Type DL, 4-cylinder, 2765 cc, water-cooled diesel developing 72 bhp at 3600 rpm Torque 170 Nm at 2200 rpm
TRANSMISSION:	Manual, selectable 4 × 4 or 4 × 2, freewheeling front hubs Type of clutch single dry plate Number of gear ratios 5 forward, 1 reverse Transfer box 2-speed
CHASSIS AND SUSPENSION:	Box section ladder frame type, rigid axles front and rear with semi-elliptical springs and telescopic shock absorbers all round

	Fuel tank	60 litres (13.2 gallons)
	Brakes	discs front, drums rear with servo
	Steering	ball nut
	Tyres	215 SR 15
	Electrical system	12V

DIMENSIONS:	Length	3.715 m (12 ft 3 in)
	Width	1.58 m (5 ft 3 in)
	Height	1.84 m (6 ft 1 in)
	Wheelbase	2.205 m (7 ft 2¾ in)
	Track	1.32 m (4 ft 4 in)
	Turning radius	10.2 m (33 ft 6 in)
	Ground clearance	0.21 m (8 in)
	Gradient	90%
	Angle of approach/departure	47°/35°

MANUFACTURER: Daihatsu Kogyo Co. Ltd., Ikeda City, Osaka, Japan

CONFIGURATION: 4 × 4, front-engined open body with canvas top, station wagon

	doors	seats	unladen weight	max load
F-80V station wagon	2	2	1290 kg (2844 lb)	490 kg (1080 lb)
F-70 soft top	2	2	1405 kg (3097 lb)	500 kg (1102 lb)

DAIHATSU F-20 SERIES

MANUFACTURER: Daihatsu Kogyo Co. Ltd., Ikeda City, Osaka, Japan

CONFIGURATION:

	doors	seats	unladen weight
F-20	2	6	1115 kg (2458 lb)
F-20	2	6	1165 kg (2568 lb)
			(station wagon)
F-25	2	10	1310 kg (2888 lb)

ENGINE: (F-20) 12R 4-cylinder, 1587 cc, water-cooled, in-line petrol developing 68 hp at 5200 rpm

TRANSMISSION:

Manual	
Type of clutch	single dry plate
Number of gear ratios	4 forward, 1 reverse/
	5 forward, 1 reverse
Transfer box	2-speed

CHASSIS AND SUSPENSION: Unitary body with subframes, rigid axles front and rear with leaf springs. Telescopic shock absorbers all round

Fuel tank	50 litres (11 gallons)
Brakes	power assisted discs at front, drums at rear, mechanical parking brake on transmission shaft
Steering	circulating ball
Tyres	6.00 ×16
Electrical system	12V

DIMENSIONS:

Length	3.485 m (11 ft 5 in)
	(F-20 4.275 m (14 ft))
Width	1.49 m (4 ft 11 in)
Height	1.82 m (6 ft)
Wheelbase	2.025 m (6 ft 8 in)
	(F-25 2.7 m (8 ft 10 in))
Track	1.21 m (4 ft)
Turning radius	5.15 m (17 ft)
Ground clearance	0.25 m (10 in)

PERFORMANCE:

Max speed	110 km/h (68 mph)
Power-to-weight ratio	16.4 kg/hp (36.16 lb/hp)
Fuel consumption	10 litres/100 km (2.2 gallons/62 miles)

ENGINE: (F-60/65) Toyota DL, 4-cylinder, 2765 cc diesel developing 69 hp at 3600 rpm

5-speed only	
Max speed	120 km/h (75 mph)
Power-to-weight ratio	18.2 kg/hp (40.12 lb/hp)
Fuel consumption	8.5–11 litres/100 km (1.87–2.42 gallons/62 miles)

DAIHATSU MIRA

MANUFACTURER: Daihatsu Kogyo Co. Ltd., Ikeda City, Osaka, Japan

CONFIGURATION: 4 ×4 front-engined hatchback saloon

	doors	seats	unladen weight
Mira	3	4	635 kg (1400 lb)

ENGINE: 2-cylinder, 548 cc, water-cooled petrol developing 30 hp at 6000 rpm

Torque	41 Nm at 3500 rpm
Compression ratio	9.2:1

TRANSMISSION:

Manual, selectable 4 ×2 or 4 ×4	
Type of clutch	single dry plate
Number of gear ratios	4 forward, 1 reverse

CHASSIS AND SUSPENSION: Unitary construction

Fuel tank	28 litres (6.16 gallons)
Brakes	drums all round, front discs with servo optional
Steering	rack and pinion
Tyres	6.95 ×12
Electrical system	12V

DIMENSIONS:

Length	3.195 m (10 ft 6 in)
Width	1.395 m (4 ft 7 in)
Height	1.36 m (4 ft 5 in)
Wheelbase	2.15 m (7 ft 1 in)
Track	1.205 m/1.21 m (rear) (3 ft 11 in/4 ft)
Turning radius	4.5 m (15 ft)
Ground clearance	0.175 m (7 in)

PERFORMANCE:

Max speed	100 km/h (62 mph)
Power-to-weight ratio	20.2 kg/hp (44.53 lb/hp)
Fuel consumption	6–9 litres/100 km (1.32–1.99 gallons/62 miles)

DODGE RAMCHARGER

No existing company has a longer pedigree than Dodge and the Ramcharger represents the last glorious fling of an industry which, in some areas at least, has still not come to grips with the high energy costs of the eighties. If the Range Rover has a rival, this vehicle, the offspring of a long line of tough off road pick-ups and Power Wagons, must be it.

MANUFACTURER:	Dodge Division, Chrysler Corporation, Detroit, Michigan, USA			
CONFIGURATION:	4 × 4, front-engined station wagon, pick-up			
	doors	**seats**	**unladen weight**	**max load**
AW150	3	5	2130 kg (4696 lb)	750 kg (1654 lb)

ENGINE:	i) V-8, 5210 cc, water-cooled petrol developing 152 hp at 4400 rpm	
	Torque	346 Nm at 2000 rpm
	Compression ratio	8.5:1
	ii) V-8, 5898 cc, water-cooled petrol developing 177 hp at 4000 rpm	
	Torque	353 Nm at 2000 rpm
	Compression ratio	8.0:1

TRANSMISSION:	Manual or 3-speed automatic	
	Number of gear ratios (manual)	4 forward, 1 reverse
	Transfer box	2-speed

CHASSIS AND SUSPENSION:	Ladder frame type. Rigid axles front and rear with semi-elliptical leaf springs all round	
	Fuel tank	132 litres (29 gallons)
	Brakes	discs front, drums rear with servo
	Steering	recirculating ball
	Tyres	235/75R 15
	Electrical system	12V

DIMENSIONS:	Length	4.68 m (15 ft 5 in)
	Width	2.02 m (6 ft 8 in)
	Height	1.91 m (6 ft 3 in)
	Wheelbase	2.69 m (8 ft 9 in)
	Track	1.67 m (5 ft 6 in)
	Turning radius	6 m (19 ft 8 in)
	Ground clearance	0.20 m (8 in)

PERFORMANCE:	(V-8, 5.2 litres)	
	Max speed	140 km/h (87 mph)
	Power-to-weight ratio	12.6 kg/hp (27.8 lb/hp)
	Fuel consumption	14–15 litres/100 km (3–5.5 gallons/62 miles)

PERFORMANCE:	(V-8, 5.9 litres)	
	Max speed	160 km/h (99 mph)
	Power-to-weight ratio	9.8 kg/hp (21.6 lb/hp)
	Fuel consumption	16–24 litres/100 km (3.5–5.3 gallons/62 miles)

Dodge Ramcharger

DELTA MINI CRUISER/EXPLORER

Philippine Police Delta Explorer

The postwar Philippine armed forces used a variety of US and Japanese supplied light vehicles and produced light armoured versions for internal security duties of US M606 Jeeps supplied under Military Assistance Programs. Then in 1972 the Philippine armed forces contracted with the Delta Motor Company of Manila to produce an indigenously developed, light 4 × 4 vehicle using the same engine as the Toyota Corona passenger car already built under licence. The chassis layout is conventional with a five-cross member channel section girder type chassis and all-steel body with more deference shown to Japanese than US styling. The cargo section has two two-person bench seats running down either side, the canvas top folds away and the windscreen folds down on to the bonnet. There are versions for ambulance, police and weapons platform variants and the Mini Cruiser serves with the armed forces of the Philippines, Qatar and the UAE. In 1983 the vehicle was renamed the Explorer.

MANUFACTURER:	Delta Motor Corporation, Manila, Philippines				
CONFIGURATION:	4 × 4, front-engined, open body with canvas top				
		doors	seats	unladen weight	max load
	RJ-2B	–	1–5	1070 kg (2359 lb)	680 kg (1499 lb)
	DJ-2B	–	2–5	1220 kg (2690 lb)	520 kg (1146 lb)
ENGINE:	i) (RJ-2B) Toyota 12RM 4-cylinder, 1587 cc, water-cooled petrol developing 90 bhp at 5400 rpm ii) (DJ-2B) Isuzu C-190 4-cylinder, water-cooled diesel developing 55 bhp at 4000 rpm				
TRANSMISSION:	Manual				
	Type of clutch		single dry plate		
	Number of gear ratios		4 forward, 1 reverse		
	Transfer box		2-speed		
CHASSIS AND SUSPENSION:	Channel section ladder type, steel body, semi-elliptical leaf springs all round with telescopic shock absorbers				
	Fuel tank		45 litres (9.9 gallons)		
	Brakes		drums all round		
	Steering		recirculating ball		
	Tyres		6.00 × 16		
	Electrical system		12V		
DIMENSIONS:	Length		3.575 m (11 ft 9 in)		
	Width		1.595 m (5 ft 3 in)		
	Height		1.925 m (6 ft 4 in)		
	Wheelbase		2.185 m (7 ft 2 in)		
	Track		1.3155 m/1.2693 m (rear) (4 ft 4 in/4 ft 2 in)		
	Turning radius		4.75 m (16 ft)		
	Ground clearance		0.215 m (8 in)		
	Angle of approach/departure		52°/39°		
PERFORMANCE:	Max speed		95 km/h (59 mph)		

ENGESA EE-34

The all-Brazilian designed and built Engesa EE-34

This prototype military vehicle was developed by the Brazilian Engesa company in 1980. Production began in 1982 and the vehicle serves with the Brazilian armed forces. Optional equipment includes a Perkins or Mercedes-Benz diesel, automatic transmission and power steering.

MANUFACTURER:	Engesa, São Paulo, Brazil			
CONFIGURATION:	4 × 4, front-engined, open body with canvas top			
	doors	seats	unladen weight	max load
	2	5	1895 kg (4178 lb)	750 kg (1653 lb)
ENGINE:	i) Mercedes-Benz OM-314 6-cylinder, water-cooled diesel			
	ii) Perkins 4.236 6-cylinder, water-cooled diesel			
TRANSMISSION:	Manual			
	Type of clutch	single dry plate		
	Number of gear ratios	4 forward, 1 reverse		
	Transfer box	2-speed		
CHASSIS AND SUSPENSION:	Box section ladder type with steel body. Leaf springs all round with hydraulic shock absorbers			
	Brakes	discs front, drums rear		
	Tyres	10.00 × 15		
	Electrical system	12V		
DIMENSIONS:	Length	4.12 m (13 ft 6 in)		
	Width	1.89 m (6 ft 2 in)		
	Height	2.025 m (6 ft 8 in)		
	Wheelbase	2.4 m (7 ft 10 in)		
	Track	1.56 m/1.55 m (rear) (5 ft 1 in/5 ft 1 in)		
	Ground clearance	0.36 m (1 ft 2 in)		
	Gradient	60%		
	Angle of approach/departure	37°/35°		

FIAT OM LEONCINO

This entirely conventional four-wheel drive light truck was adopted as the Italian Army's standard 1000 kg load carrier in the late 1960s. The engine is front mounted in a conventional chassis with a soft top cab and rear load area with removable canvas cover but no drop sides or tailgate. Known officially as the 'Autocarro Leggero 1 Tonellata, 4 × 4 Leoncino' the vehicle serves with the Italian Army with a payload in excess of one tonne off roads and 1500 kg on the highway. Maximum towed load cross-country is two tonnes.

MANUFACTURER:	FIAT OM, Brescia, Italy			
CONFIGURATION:	4 × 4, front-engined truck, soft top cab with removable doors			
	doors	seats	unladen weight	max load
	2	1 +2	2860 kg (6305 lb)	1500 kg (3307 lb) (on road)
ENGINE:	CO2D/12, 4-cylinder diesel developing 85 hp at 2400 rpm			
TRANSMISSION:	Manual			
	Type of clutch	single dry plate		
	Number of gear ratios	5 forward, 1 reverse		
	Transfer box	2-speed		
CHASSIS AND SUSPENSION:	Channel section ladder type frame, semi-elliptical springs with hydraulic shock absorbers			
	Fuel tank	90 litres (19.8 gallons)		
	Brakes	dual circuit hydraulic, mechanical parking		
	Tyres	9.00 × 16		
	Electrical system	24V		
DIMENSIONS:	Length	4.45 m (14 ft 7 in)		
	Width	2 m (6 ft 7 in)		
	Height	2.13 m (6 ft 11 in)		
	Wheelbase	2.5 m (8 ft 3 in)		
	Track	1.63 m/1.67 m (5 ft 4 in/5 ft 5 in)		
	Turning radius	5.2 m (17 ft)		
	Ground clearance	0.24 m (8 in)		
	Gradient	60%		
PERFORMANCE:	Max speed	76.6 km/h (47.5 mph)		
	Power-to-weight ratio	33.6 kg/hp (74 lb/hp)		
	Fuel consumption	18 litres/100 km (3.96 gallons/62 miles)		

FIAT CAMPAGNOLA 1107 AD

Fiat 2500 Campagnola Diesel

Produced for both the military and civil markets since 1974, the Fiat Campagnola supplanted the original Fiat AR-59 (see p. 56) Jeep-type vehicle which had been in production for the Italian army since 1951 and manufactured under licence in Yugoslavia as the Zastava AR-51. The Red Flag factory at Kragujevac has kept in step with Fiat and now also builds the 1107 AD.

The Campagnola comes in long and short wheelbase versions with hard or soft canvas tops or station wagon enclosed body, with petrol or diesel engines, and in military service it is readily adaptable to specialised and ambulance roles. Desert versions come with special air and fuel filters, sealed clutch bearings, grille guards and a low-octane fuel engine. Both civil and military versions have heater, defrost and ventilation, fire extinguisher, front towing eyes, rear towing hook, fuel cans, pick and shovel as standard equipment.

ENGINE:	i) 6132 AZ 2000 4-cylinder, 2-litre, water-cooled petrol developing 80 hp at 4600 rpm ii) Sofim 8142.61, 4-cylinder, 2.4-litre, water-cooled developing 72 hp at 2400 rpm
TRANSMISSION:	Manual
	Type of clutch — single dry plate
	Number of gear ratios — 5 forward, 1 reverse
	Transfer box — 2-speed
CHASSIS AND SUSPENSION:	Unitary construction, independent McPherson type all round with longitudinal torsion bar, single telescopic shock absorbers at front and twin at rear
	Fuel tank — 57 litres (12.54 gallons)
	Brakes — dual circuit hydraulic with servo-assisted drums all round
	Steering — hourglass and roller (power assist on diesel)
	Tyres — 4 and 1 spare, 7.00 ×16
	Electrical system — 24V
DIMENSIONS:	Length — 3.775 m (12 ft 5 in)
	Width — 1.58 m (5 ft 2 in)
	Height — 1.901 m (6 ft 3 in)
	Wheelbase — 2.3 m (7 ft 6 in)
	Track — 1.365 m (4 ft 6 in) (front), 1.404 m (4 ft 7 in) (rear)
	Turning radius — 5.4 m (18 ft)
	Ground clearance — 0.27 m (11 in)
	Fording — 0.7 m (2 ft 4 in)
	Gradient — 60%
	Angle of approach/departure — 44°/55°
PERFORMANCE:	(1107 petrol)
	Max speed — 120 km/h (75 mph)
	Power-to-weight ratio — 20.9 kg/hp (46.08 lb/hp)
	Fuel consumption — 12.5–16.8 litres/100 km (2.75–3.69 gallons/62 miles)
PERFORMANCE:	(2500 diesel)
	Max speed — 115 km/h (71 mph)
	Power-to-weight ratio — 25.3 kg/hp (55.78 lb/hp)
	Fuel consumption — 12.5–15.3 litres/100 km (2.75–3.37 gallons/62 miles)

MANUFACTURER: FIAT, Direzione Mezzi Speciali, Turin, Italy

CONFIGURATION: 4 ×4, front-engined, open body with canvas/hard top station wagon

	doors	seats	unladen weight	max load
1107 Ad (canvas top)				
	2	3 +4	1670 kg (3682 lb)	750 kg (1653 lb)
1107 AD (Lwb with hard top)				
	2	3 +6	1760 kg (3880 lb)	750 kg (1653 lb)
2500 Diesel				
	2		1820 kg (4012 lb)	750 kg (1653 lb)

FIAT PANDA

The diminutive Fiat Panda 4 × 4, launched in 1984

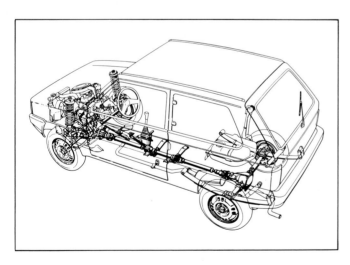

Fiat saw a slot in the four-wheel drive market right at the bottom and in 1983/4 launched the diminuitive 4 × 4 Panda at a price below the Suzuki SJ 410 series and the Lada Niva. Engineering was developed in conjunction with Steyr-Daimler-Puch and as Fiat themselves point out 'the car does not profess to be a Range Rover or a Land-cruiser but it will perform many of the tasks of these vehicles in fine style, with economy and comfort'. First gear is a crawler gear 25 per cent lower than normal. The Panda is the world's first transverse engine 4 × 4 and has a three piece propeller shaft, while rear suspension and braking differ from the standard Panda.

MANUFACTURER:	FIAT, Turin, Italy			
CONFIGURATION:	4 × 4, saloon car			
	doors	seats	unladen weight	max load
	3	5	740 kg (1631 lb)	400 kg (882 lb)
ENGINE:	Fiat A12 4-cylinder, 965 cc, water-cooled petrol developing 48 hp at 5600 rpm			
	Torque		70 Nm at 3500 rpm	
	Compression ratio		9.2:1	
TRANSMISSION:	Manual			
	Number of gear ratios		5 forward, 1 reverse	
	1) 3.909:1	2) 2.055:1	3) 1.342:1	4) 0.964:1
	5) 0.723:1	Rev. 3.615:1		
	Final drive		5.455:1	
CHASSIS AND SUSPENSION:	Unitary construction. Independent front suspension via coil springs, rigid rear axle with semi-elliptical springs and telescopic shock absorbers			
	Fuel tank		35 litres (7.69 gallons)	
	Steering		rack and pinion	
	Tyres		145 SR 13	
	Electrical system		12V	
DIMENSIONS:	Length		3.39 m (11 ft 1 in)	
	Width		1.485 m (4 ft 10 in)	
	Height		1.46 m (4 ft 9 in)	
	Wheelbase		2.17 m (7 ft 1 in)	
	Track		1.255 m/1.26 m (rear) (4 ft 1 in/4 ft 2 in)	
	Turning radius		4.6 m (15 ft)	
	Ground clearance		0.18 m (7 in)	
PERFORMANCE:	Max speed		135 km/h (84 mph)	
	Power-to-weight ratio		15.4 kg/hp (33.95 lb/hp)	
	Fuel consumption		5.9–7.9 litres/100 km (1.29–1.73 gallons/62 miles)	

FIAT AR-59

During the Second World War the Italian Army largely depended on open militarised versions of standard vehicles as field cars (*torpedo militare*).

The post-war Italian Army, a part of NATO from 1949, generated a requirement for new tactical vehicles and in 1950 Alfa Romeo and Fiat produced prototypes for quarter-tonne 4 × 4 light vehicles. Both eventually went into production for civil and military purposes. The Alfa vehicle, the AR 52 'Matta' with an 1884 cc four-cylinder engine was only in production from 1952–55 but the Fiat model, the AR-51 (AR stands for *Autovettura da Ricognizione*, reconnaissance vehicle) remained in production through three variants until 1974 when it was replaced by the Fiat 1107 AD.

The original AR-51 was powered by a four-cylinder petrol engine developing 53 hp giving the vehicle a maximum road speed of 100 km/h (62 mph). From 1953 a 1901 cc, 43 hp, Fiat diesel engine was offered as an option and, on the civil market, the AR-51 was available as the 'Campagnola' and in various applications including snow plough, fire appliance, station wagon and so on.

In 1955 it was replaced in production by the AR-55 with a more powerful engine developing 59 hp and by the AR-59 in 1959 with a 63 hp engine.

The layout of the AR-59 is of the conventional Jeep-type with folding windscreen and canvas top. The doors can be swung back and clipped flush with the body if required. Driver and co-driver have individual seats with bench seats for four in the rear. Military vehicles have been adapted as platforms for recoilless rifles and rocket launchers. The AR-59 can carry 480 kg (1058 lb) of cargo or a 500 kg (1102 lb) trailer although they are frequently used to tow the much heavier OTO Melara 105 mm pack howitzer.

The Crvena Zastava (Red Flag) factory at Kragujevac, Yugoslavia built the AR-59 under licence as the Zastava AR-51.

MANUFACTURER:	FIAT, Turin, Italy			
CONFIGURATION:	4 × 4, front-engined, open body with canvas cover			
		doors	seats	unladen weight	max load
	AR-59	2	1 + 5	1440 kg (3175 lb)	480 kg (1058 lb)
ENGINE:	Model 105 4-cylinder, 1901 cc, water-cooled petrol developing 56 hp at 4000 rpm, diesel optional			
TRANSMISSION:	Manual			
	Type of clutch	single dry plate		
	Number of gear ratios	4 forward, 1 reverse		
	Transfer box	2-speed		
CHASSIS AND SUSPENSION:	Ladder frame box section chassis with steel body. Independent front suspension via coil springs, rear leaf springs			
	Brakes	drums all round, hydraulic, mechanical parking		
	Tyres	6.40 × 16		
	Electrical system	24V		
DIMENSIONS:	Length	3.596 m (11 ft 10 in)		
	Width	1.57 m (5 ft 2 in)		
	Height	1.8 m (5 ft 11 in)		
	Wheelbase	2.25 m (7 ft 5 in)		
	Track	1.254 m/1.26 m (rear) (4 ft 1 in/4 ft 2 in (rear))		
	Turning radius	5.4 m (18 ft)		
	Ground clearance	0.2 m (8 in)		
	Fording	0.6 m (2 ft)		
	Gradient	89%		
	Angle of approach/departure	60°/35°		
PERFORMANCE:	Max speed	110 km/h (68 mph)		
	Operating range	450 km (280 miles)		

FORD U-50

Ford of Brazil produced the U-50 until the early 1980s in both civil and military forms, the civil version available in 2.057 and 2.565 m wheelbases. The vehicle is virtually identical to the M38A1.

MANUFACTURER:	Ford Do Brasil, São Paulo, Brazil			
CONFIGURATION:	4 × 4, front-engined, open body with canvas top			
		doors	seats	unladen weight	max load
	U-50	–	1 + 3	1167 kg (2573 lb)	540 kg (1190 lb)
ENGINE:	Ford 4-cylinder, 2.3-litre, water-cooled petrol developing 91 hp at 5000 rpm			
TRANSMISSION:	Manual			
	Number of gear ratios	4 forward, 1 reverse		
	Transfer box	2-speed		
CHASSIS AND SUSPENSION:	Fuel tank	50 litres (10.99 gallons)		
	Brakes	drums all round		
	Steering	worm and roller		
	Tyres	6.00 × 16		
	Electrical system	12V or 24V		
DIMENSIONS:	Length	3.509 m (11 ft 6 in)		
	Width	1.521 m (5 ft)		
	Height	1.82 m (6 ft)		
	Wheelbase	2.057 m (6 ft 9 in)		
	Track	1.234 m/1.232 m (rear) (4 ft/4 ft)		
	Turning radius	6 m (20 ft)		
	Ground clearance	0.203 m (8 in)		
	Fording	0.35 m (1 ft 2 in)		
	Gradient	100%		
	Angle of approach/departure	35°/29°		
PERFORMANCE:	Max speed	125 km/h (78 mph)		

FORD BRONCO

The first Ford Bronco arrived in 1966 in an attempt to do for the US off-road market what the Mustang had failed to do for the sports car market, that is claw back sales from European competition. But like the Mustang it made a market of its own and an altogether new awareness of off-roading with the marketing muscle of Ford behind it which the existing competition, AMC and International Harvester, could not have provided.

The Bronco II is a rationalised and repackaged exercise in the same market following the down-sized Chevy Blazer launched in the 1983 model year. The full size Bronco continues with a range of engine, transmission and trim options.

MANUFACTURER: Ford Motor Company, Detroit, Michigan, USA

CONFIGURATION: 4 × 4, front-engined, station wagon

	doors	seats	unladen weight	max load
Bronco	3	2–6	1935 kg (4266 lb)	700 kg (4543 lb)

ENGINE:
i) 6-cylinder, 4918 cc, water-cooled petrol developing 117 hp at 4000 rpm
Torque 260 Nm at 1800 rpm
Compression ratio 8:1
ii) V-8, 4942 cc, water-cooled petrol developing 139 hp at 3600 rpm
Torque 315 Nm at 1600 rpm
Compression ratio 8.4:1
iii) V-8, 5766 cc, water-cooled petrol developing 143 hp at 3400 rpm
Torque 360 Nm at 2000 rpm
Compression ratio 8.3:1

TRANSMISSION:
Manual or automatic
Type of clutch single dry plate
Number of gear ratios 4 forward, 1 reverse (Manual)
1) 6.69:1 2) 3.34:1 3) 1.66:1 4) 1:1
Rev. 8.26:1
Transfer box 2-speed

CHASSIS AND SUSPENSION: Box section ladder type with steel body. Independent front suspension with coil springs. Rigid rear axle with semi-elliptical leaf springs, telescopic shock absorbers all round

Fuel tank 95 litres (20.89 gallons)
Brakes discs front, drums rear with servo
Steering
Tyres 215/75-16
Electrical system 12V

DIMENSIONS:
Length 4.51 m (14 ft 9 in)
Width 1.96 m (6 ft 5 in)
Height 1.86 m (6 ft 1 in)
Wheelbase 2.66 m (8 ft 9 in)
Track 1.655 m/1.635 m (rear) (5 ft 5 in/5 ft 4 in)
Turning radius 5.7 m (19 ft)
Ground clearance 0.2 m (8 in)

PERFORMANCE:
6-cylinder 4.9-litre petrol
Max speed 130 km/h (81 mph)
Power-to-weight ratio 16.5 kg/hp (36.37 lb/hp)
Fuel consumption 14–20 litres/100 km (3.07–4.39 gallons/62 miles)

V-8 5.8-litre petrol
Max speed 145–155 km/h (90–96 mph)
Power-to-weight ratio 14.6 kg/hp (32.18 lb/hp)
Fuel consumption 15–24 litres/100 km (3.29–5.27 gallons/62 miles)

FORD BRONCO II

MANUFACTURER: Ford Motor Company, Detroit, Michigan, USA

CONFIGURATION: 4 × 4, front-engined, station wagon

	doors	seats	unladen weight
Bronco II	3	4–5	1400 kg (3085 lb)

ENGINE: V-6, 2792 cc, water-cooled petrol developing 117 hp at 4600 rpm
Torque 203 Nm at 2600 rpm
Compression ratio 8.7:1

TRANSMISSION:
Manual, selection 4 × 4 or 4 × 2, optional locking differential
Type of clutch single dry plate
Number of gear ratios i) 4 forward, 1 reverse
1) 3.96:1 2) 2.08:1 3) 1.39:1 4) 1:1
Rev. 3.39:1 Final drive 3.08:1/3.73:1
ii) 5 forward, 1 reverse
1) 3.96:1 2) 2.08:1 3) 1.39:1 4) 1:1 5) 0.84:1
Rev. 3.39:1 Final drive 3.45:1/3.73:1
iii) Automatic with 3 speeds
Transfer box 2-speed 1:1/2.48:1

CHASSIS AND SUSPENSION: Box section ladder type with steel body. Independent front suspension by coil springs. Rigid rear axle with semi-elliptical leaf springs, telescopic shock absorbers all round

Fuel tank 64.5 litres (14.18 gallons)
Brakes discs front, drums rear
Tyres 195/75 R × 15
Electrical system 12V

DIMENSIONS:
Length 4.025 m (13 ft 2 in)
Width 1.65 m (5 ft 5 in)
Wheelbase 2.39 m (7 ft 10 in)
Track 1.435 m (4 ft 8 in)
Turning radius 5.75 m (19 ft)
Ground clearance 0.2 (8 in)

PERFORMANCE:
Max speed 145 km/h (90 mph)
Power-to-weight ratio 12 kg/hp (26.45 lb/hp)
Fuel consumption 12–19 litres/100 km (2.63–4.17 gallons/62 miles)

Main picture: The crisply styled down sized '84 Ford Bronco II.
Inset: The bigger Bronco carries the Ford flag in the full size, four
wheel drive wagon market

FORD RANGER

The Ranger is Ford's contender in the lively US 4 × 4 pick-up market

The Ranger is Ford of America's contender in the four-wheel drive pick-up market displaying typical US styling, driver comforts and engineering innovation including independent suspension via so called 'twin-traction beams' and coil springs. The front hubs are manually unlockable for 4 × 2 running and drive train options include four or five speed manual transmission with 2.3-litre petrol engine, four or five speed manual or automatic with a 2.8-litre V-6 petrol engine which also features an electronic engine control system.

A special snow plough package is available featuring heavy duty front springs and beefed up shock absorbers all round.

MANUFACTURER:	Ford Motor Company, Detroit, Michigan, USA

CONFIGURATION: 4 × 4, front-engined pick-up with steel cab

	doors	seats	max loaded weight
Swb	2	2	2000 kg (4420 lb)
Lwb	2	2	2030 kg (4480 lb)

ENGINE:	i) 4-cylinder, 2.3-litre, water-cooled petrol
	ii) V-6, 2.8-litre, water-cooled petrol

TRANSMISSION:	Manual, automatic optional. Selectable 4 × 4 or 4 × 2, freewheeling front hubs
Number of gear ratios	i) 4 forward, 1 reverse
	ii) 5 forward, 1 reverse (2.8 litre)
Transfer box	2-speed

CHASSIS AND SUSPENSION:	Box section ladder type. Coil springs front, semi-elliptical leaf springs rear, telescopic shock absorbers all round
Fuel tank	130 litres (30 gallons)
Brakes	discs front, drums rear with power assist
Tyres	15 × 5.0
Electrical system	12V

DIMENSIONS:	swb	
	Length	4.4 m (14 ft 7 in)
	Width	1.67 m (5 ft 6 in)
	Height	1.70 m (5 ft 7 in)
	Wheelbase	2.74 m (9 ft)
	Track	1.45 m/1.41 m (4 ft 8 in/4 ft 7 in)
	Turning radius	11.3 m (37 ft)
	Ground clearance	0.19 m (6¾ in)
	lwb	
	Length	4.8 m (15 ft 8 in)
	Width	1.67 m (5 ft 6 in)
	Height	1.70 m (5 ft 7 in)
	Wheelbase	2.74 m (9 ft 6 in)

FORD/AMC M151 SERIES

In 1950, with the Korean War at its height, research began at the US Ordnance Tank Automotive Command for an entirely new 'military, utility tactical truck'. The resulting 'Mutt' was a long time in coming – from the first prototypes in 1952 to production in 1960. The Ford Motor Company won the original development contract and the resulting XM151 prototype was in fact completely different to the Willys vehicles that had gone before, if in general external appearance it looked like a linear descendant. Experimental prototypes were built and tested with separate chassis and rigid axles, and with a unitary body with independent suspension all round, and this design was eventually adopted. Prototypes were also built in steel and in light alloy but the steel bodies XM151E1 was the base model chosen for production at Ford's Highland Park plant.

In 1964 the M151 was supplanted by the M151A1 with improved suspension and in 1970 by the M151A2 with a completely redesigned rear suspension which at last eliminated the vehicle's tendency to oversteer. Designated the M151A2, many of these improved vehicles, which also featured revised lighting and collapsible steering wheels, were manufactured by the AM General, successor company to Kaiser-Jeep and Willys Motors.

There have been several variants of the basic model – the M151A2LC with a two-speed transfer box (the standard model has a single-speed transfer box with four forward and one reverse gears with selectable 4 × 4 or 4 × 2 drive). The M151AC mounted a recoilless rifle while the experimental XM408 and XM384 were 'stretched' 6 × 6 and 8 × 8 versions. The M107 and M108 are dedicated radio versions with the operator's seat facing rearwards and the M718A1 is an ambulance version with a crew of two and room for two stretchers and two seated patients or three stretchers. The M825 is a weapons carrier with mounting provisions for the M40 106 mm recoilless rifle and revised positions for the spare tyre and jerry cans. This system is being replaced by the TOW anti-tank missile.

There are many options including personnel heater kit, arctic winterisation kit, deep water fording kit for depths up to 1.52 metres (5 feet), power brakes, 100-amp heavy duty alternator, searchlight, front-mounted winch, solar reflective paint and quarter-ton trailer.

The M151 serves with the US Army, Air Force and Marines and over 100 other countries with nearly 100,000 manufactured. The M151A2, the M718A1 ambulance and M825 weapons carrier are available from AM General on a requirement basis.

MANUFACTURER:	AM General Corporation, Detroit, Michigan, USA			
CONFIGURATION:	4 × 4, front-engined, open body with canvas top			
		doors	seats	unladen weight	max load
	M151A2 –	4	1107 kg (2440 lb)	544 kg (1199 lb)
	M718A1 –	2	1247 kg (2749 lb)	
ENGINE:	L-142 4-cylinder, 2320 cc, water-cooled petrol developing 72 hp at 4000 rpm			
TRANSMISSION:	Manual, selectable 4 × 4 or 4 × 2			
	Type of clutch	single dry plate		
	Number of gear ratios	4 forward, 1 reverse		
	Transfer box	1-speed integral with transmission		
CHASSIS AND SUSPENSION:	Unitary construction with subframes, independent suspension all round via coil springs and hydraulic shock absorbers (M825 has additional coil springs on rear axles)			
	Fuel tank	56 litres (12.32 gallons)		
	Steering	worm and double roller		
	Tyres	7.00 × 16		
	Electrical system	24V		
DIMENSIONS:	Length	3.371 m (11 ft 1 in)		
	Width	1.633 m (5 ft 4 in)		
	Height	1.803 m (5 ft 11 in)		
	Wheelbase	2.159 m (7 ft 1 in)		
	Track	1.346 m (4 ft 5 in)		
	Turning radius	5.638 m (18 ft)		
	Ground clearance	0.26 m (10 in)		
	Fording	0.533 m (1 ft 9 in) (with kit) 1.524 m (5 ft)		
	Gradient	75%		
	Angle of approach/departure	66°/37°		
PERFORMANCE:	Max speed	90 km/h (56 mph)		

The M151A2 is available from AM General
according to customer requirement

GAZ-69,69A (UAZ-69,-69A)

GAZ-69A photographed in South America

Produced in very large numbers and still in widespread service with Soviet and Warsaw Pact armed forces, Middle East and Soviet client states, the GAZ-69 and its derivatives are among the most ubiquitous of military four-wheel drive light vehicles.

The Gorki'y Automobil Zavod (Gorky motor vehicle factory) produced a Jeep-type field car, the GAZ-67, from 1942 onwards and this stayed in production until supplanted in 1952 by the GAZ-69.

The layout was entirely conventional with a ladder frame chassis, water-cooled engine and beam axles sprung by longitudinal semi-elliptical leaf springs.

There were two basic models, the GAZ-69 with two doors and bench seats down each side of the rear cargo compartment and the four-door GAZ-69A with transverse seats, with the spare wheel carried under the rear of the vehicle rather than on the left side of the body.

In 1956 production switched to the Ul'yanovsk plant (UAZ prefix) where manufacture continued until 1973. Later versions were the UAZ-69M which had a 65 hp (M-2) engine rather than the 55 hp of the original.

Variants include the GAZ-46 MAV (small amphibious truck) derived in outline from the wartime Ford GPA, a mine detector vehicle and anti-tank missile launcher with four Snapper wire-guided ATGWs on rail launchers behind a folding canvas cover, the cab itself protected by a firewall pierced by a viewing window.

A version of the vehicle is built in North Korea with a modified front end with headlights incorporated into full width front wings and in Romania from 1964 onwards at the Uzina Mecanica Muscel (UMM), under the designation M-461, equipped with a four-speed gearbox.

MANUFACTURER: Gorki'y Automobil Zavod, USSR

CONFIGURATION: 4 × 4, front-engined, open body with canvas top

	doors	seats	unladen weight	max load
69	2	6	1525 kg (3362 lb)	650 kg (1433 lb)
69A	4	6	1535 kg (3384 lb)	425 kg (937 lb)

ENGINE: M-20, 4-cylinder, water-cooled petrol developing 52 hp at 3600 rpm

TRANSMISSION: Manual

Type of clutch	single dry plate
Number of gear ratios	3 forward, 1 reverse
Transfer box	2-speed

CHASSIS AND SUSPENSION: Ladder type chassis frame. Semi-elliptical springs with double-acting hydraulic shock absorbers all round

Fuel tank	75 litres/60 litres (GAZ 69A) (16.5 gallons/13.2 gallons (GAZ 69A))
Brakes	drums all round
Steering	globoid worm
Tyres	6.50 × 16
Electrical system	12V

DIMENSIONS:

i) GAZ 69

Length	3.85 m (12 ft 8 in)
Width	1.85 m (6 ft 1 in)
Height	2.03 m (6 ft 8 in)
Wheelbase	2.3 m (7 ft 6 in)
Track	1.44 m (4 ft 8 in)
Turning radius	6 m (19 ft 8½ in)
Ground clearance	0.21 m (8 in)
Fording	0.55 m (1 ft 10 in)
Gradient	60%
Angle of approach/departure	45°/35°

ii) GAZ 69A

Length	3.85 m (12 ft 8 in)
Width	1.75 m (5 ft 8 in)
Height	1.92 m (6 ft 4 in)
Wheelbase	2.3 m (7 ft 6 in)
Track	1.44 m (4 ft 8 in)
Turning radius	6.5 m (21 ft 4 in)
Ground clearance	0.21 m (8 in)
Fording	0.55 m (1 ft 10 in)
Gradient	60%
Angle of approach/departure	45°/35°

PERFORMANCE:

Max speed	90 km/h (56 mph)
Fuel consumption	14 litres/100 km at 40 km/h (3.08 gallons/68 miles at 25 mph)

HOTCHKISS M201

M201, workhorse of the French Army for 30 years

A veteran of France's military campaigns from Indo-China in 1954 to Tchad in 1983, the M201 remains the standard light vehicle of the French Army, over 40,000 being manufactured under licence from Willys between 1953 and 1969 by Hotchkiss who abandoned civil motor manufacture in 1956.

Based directly on the Willys MB but with minor differences in carburation, electrics, wheels etc, the M201 has appeared in many variants including special desert models, and mounting recoilless rifles or anti-tank guided weapons, these vehicles having reinforced suspensions.

The vehicle is known as the VLTT in the French Army – *Véhicule de Liaison Tout Terrain*. Hotchkiss built a number of long wheelbase versions known as the HWL and also built the Willys CJ3B as the JH-101 but with a side valve engine (1955–60), and with a diesel as the JH-102 from 1961. Numbers of M201s are coming on to the surplus market as the French Army gets its replacement programme underway with the Peugeot P4, 15,000 of which are due for delivery before 1987.

MANUFACTURER:	Hotchkiss-Brandt, Paris, France			
CONFIGURATION:	4 × 4, open body with canvas top			
	doors	seats	unladen weight	max load
	–	4	1120 kg (2469 lb)	1520 kg (3351 lb)
ENGINE:	4-cylinder, water-cooled petrol developing 61 hp at 3600 rpm			
TRANSMISSION:	Manual			
	Type of clutch	single dry plate		
	Number of gear ratios	3 forward, 1 reverse		
	Transfer box	2-speed		
CHASSIS AND SUSPENSION:	Ladder type. Semi-elliptical leaf springs and hydraulic shock absorbers all round			
	Fuel tank	49 litres (10.78 gallons)		
	Brakes	drum		
	Tyres	6.50 × 16		
	Electrical system	24V		
DIMENSIONS:	Length	3.36 m (11 ft)		
	Width	1.58 m (5 ft 2 in)		
	Height	1.77 m (5 ft 10 in)		
	Wheelbase	2.03 m (6 ft 8 in)		
	Track	1.24 m (4 ft)		
	Ground clearance	0.22 m (8 in)		
	Gradient	65%		
PERFORMANCE:	Max speed	100 km/h (62 mph)		

ISUZU RODEO

The influence of the *ad hoc* styling which resulted in the
Range Rover can best be seen in this attractive Japanese
look-alike. That this diesel powered vehicle is more than
just a pretty face can well be deduced by its phenomenal
success in the Third World market. The vehicle is also
sold as the Bighorn and Trooper.

Isuzu LS Luxury Sports Trooper

Isuzu DLX Trooper

MANUFACTURER:	Isuzu, Tokyo, Japan

CONFIGURATION: 4 × 4, front-engined, open body with soft top, station wagon on 2 wheelbases

	doors	seats	unladen weight	max load
Roadster	3	5	1180 kg	770 kg
			(2601 lb)	(1697 lb)
Station wagon	3	5	1250 kg	700 kg
			(2756 lb)	(1543 lb)
Station wagon (lwb)	3	5	1290 kg	670 kg
			(2844 lb)	(1477 lb)

ENGINE: G200 4-cylinder, 1950 cc, water-cooled petrol developing 88 hp at 4600 rpm

Torque	140 Nm at 3000 rpm
Compression ratio	8.4:1

TRANSMISSION: Manual, selection 4 × 2 or 4 × 4, optional differential lock

Type of clutch	single dry plate
Number of gear ratios	4 forward, 1 reverse

1) 4.128:1   2) 2.497:1   3) 1.482:1   4) 1:1
Rev. 3.826:1

Final drive	4.555:1
Transfer box	2-speed 1.87:1/1:1

CHASSIS AND SUSPENSION: Ladder frame. Independent front suspension via torsion bars with hydraulic shock absorbers. Rigid rear axle with semi-elliptical leaf springs, hydraulic shock absorbers

Fuel tank	50 litres (10.99 gallons)
Brakes	discs front, drums rear, power assist
Steering	recirculating ball, power assist optional
Tyres	6.00 × 16
Electrical system	12V

DIMENSIONS:

swb
Length	4.07 m (13 ft 4 in)
Width	1.65 m (5 ft 5 in)
Height	1.8 m (5 ft 11 in)
Wheelbase	2.3 m (7 ft 6 in)
Track	1.34 m/1.3 m (rear) (4 ft 5 in/4 ft 3 in)
Turning radius	4.8 m (16 ft)
Ground clearance	0.22 m (9 in)

lwb
Length	4.42 m (14 ft 6 in)
Width	1.65 m (5 ft 5 in)
Height	1.8m (5 ft 11 in)
Wheelbase	2.65 m (8 ft 8 in)
Track	1.34 m/1.3 m (rear) (4 ft 5 in/4 ft 3 in)
Turning radius	4.8 m (16 ft)
Ground clearance	0.22 m (9 in)

PERFORMANCE:
Max speed	132 km/h (82 mph)
Power-to-weight ratio	13.4 kg/hp (29.54 lb/hp)
Fuel consumption	12–18 litres/100 km (2.63–3.95 gallons/62 miles)

Isuzu LS Trooper with optional electric winch

JAMY COMANDO

Like the SAFO, the Comando was developed by the Jamy company in conjunction with the Brazilian Army's Engineering Institute as a technology-proving prototype reconnaissance and command vehicle.

The Comando has a tubular frame chassis with the engine at the rear and a cut down steel body with integral roll bar. The driver's position is on the centreline with seats for commander and radio operator each side, slightly set back. Various communication sets can be installed and there is a winch mounted internally at the front of the vehicle.

Reflecting Brazil's autonomous energy supply policies, the prototype is fitted with an alcohol-burning Chevrolet engine although the vehicle is compatible with a standard diesel unit.

MANUFACTURER:	Jamy, Rio de Janeiro, Brazil		
CONFIGURATION:	4 × 4, rear-engined, open body with roll bar		
	doors	seats	unladen weight	max load
	–	1 + 2	2200 kg (4850 lb)	750 kg (1653 lb)
ENGINE:	Chevrolet 2505 6-cylinder, water-cooled, in-line alcohol developing 171 hp at 4800 rpm		
TRANSMISSION:	Automatic	
	Number of gear ratios	3 forward, 1 reverse
	Transfer box	2-speed with PTO for winch
CHASSIS AND SUSPENSION:	Space frame of tubular steel with light steel cladding. Independent suspension all round	
	Brakes	discs all round, mechanical parking
	Steering	hydraulic
	Tyres	9.00 × 10
	Electrical system	12V
DIMENSIONS:	Length	4.27 m (14 ft)
	Width	1.7 m (5 ft 7 in)
	Height	1.6 m (5 ft 3 in)
	Wheelbase	2.9 m (9 ft 6 in)
	Turning radius	6.9 m (23 ft)
	Ground clearance	0.3 m (1 ft)
	Gradient	83%
	Angle of approach/departure	70°/50°
PERFORMANCE:	Max speed	120 km/h (75 mph)
	Power-to-weight ratio	12.9 kg/hp (28.44 lb/hp)

JAMY SAFO

A technology-proving prototype for an ultra-light, all-terrain vehicle, the SAFO design shows the engineering economy and no-frills approach typical of air-portable designs.

The vehicle has been developed by the Jamy Company in conjunction with the Brazilian Army's Military Engineering Institute and is known as the *Sistema de Alta Flexibilidad Operacional* (SAFO), or High Operational Flexibility System, and is powered by a 1300 cc, water-cooled, petrol engine built by VW do Brasil.

The engine is mounted underfloor amidships leaving a flat corrugated load area, the rear half of which swings forward to rest on top of the rear decking thus reducing the overall length. The rear wheels can be unlocked and swung forward through 160 degrees, the wheels being shod in wide low-pressure tyres. The prototypes have been tested as weapons platforms with machine guns or Cobra ATGWs and trials are continuing.

MANUFACTURER:	Jamy, Rio de Janeiro, Brazil		
CONFIGURATION:	4 × 4 air-portable, open platform		
		doors	seats	unladen weight	max load
	SAFO	–	1 + 1	600 kg (1323 lb)	500 kg (1102 lb)
ENGINE:	VW do Brasil 4-cylinder, 1300 cc, water-cooled, in-line petrol developing 38 hp at 4000 rpm	
	Fuel tank	30 litres (6.6 gallons)
	Brakes	hydraulic, mechanical parking
	Electrical system	12V
DIMENSIONS:	Length	3.24 m (10 ft 8 in) (2.45 m (8 ft) folded)
	Width	1.8 m (5 ft 11 in)
	Height	1.46 m (4 ft 9 in)
	Wheelbase	1.85 m (6 ft 1 in) (0.76 m (2 ft 6 in) folded)
	Track	1.52 m/1.57 m (5 ft/5 ft 2 in)
	Angle of approach/departure	50°/55°
PERFORMANCE:	Max speed	87 km/h (54 mph)
	Power-to-weight ratio	15.7 kg/hp (34.61 lb/hp)
	Fuel consumption	20 litres/100 km (4.4 gallons/62 miles)

JEEP CHEROKEE

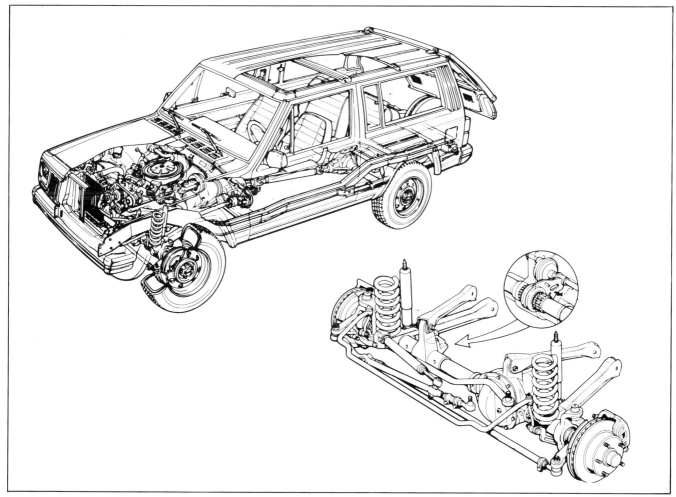

'84 Jeep Cherokee 2-door. Inset: Cherokee Front suspension showing axle disconnect

Jeep Corporation launched their new range of Cherokee four-wheel drive vehicles in 1983 after five years of development and investment in new plant. Significantly they are lighter and smaller than the vehicles they replace and crisper in styling inside and out showing the influence of the AMC-Renault corporate marketing and product development tie-up. The two-door Cherokee is made available in 'Pioneer' and 'Chief' trim packages.

MANUFACTURER: AMC Toledo, Ohio, USA

CONFIGURATION: 4 × 4, front-engined, station wagon

	doors	seats	unladen weight	max load
Turbo-diesel	3/5	5	1348 kg (2972 lb)	738 kg (1627 lb)
V-6	3/5	5	1423 kg (3137 lb)	752 kg (1658 lb)

ENGINE:
i) 4-cylinder, 2068 cc, water-cooled diesel with turbo-charging
Compression ratio   21.5:1
ii) V-6, 2837 cc, water-cooled petrol developing 111 hp at 4800 rpm
Torque   197 Nm at 2100 rpm
Compression ratio   8.5:1

TRANSMISSION: Manual or 3-speed automatic
Type of clutch   single dry plate
Number of gear ratios   5 forward, 1 reverse (manual)
1) 3.93:1   2) 2.33:1   3) 1.45:1   4) 1:1   5) 0.85:1
Rev. 3.76:1
Final drive   3.31:1/3.73:1
Transfer box   2-speed   1:1   2.61:1

CHASSIS AND SUSPENSION: Ladder frame chassis welded directly to floorpan.
Coil springs front, semi-elliptical leaf springs rear

Fuel tank   51 litres (11.21 gallons) (76.5 litres (16.82 gallons) optional)
Brakes   discs front, drums rear with servo
Steering   recirculating ball
Tyres   P205/75 R15
Electrical system   12V

DIMENSIONS:
Length   4.2 m (13 ft 9 in)
Width   1.76 m (5 ft 9 in)
Height   1.628 m (5 ft 4 in)
Wheelbase   2.576 m (8 ft 5 in)
Track   1.448 m (4 ft 9 in)
Turning radius   5.55 m (18 ft)
Ground clearance   0.222 m (9 in)
Angle of approach/departure   39.7°/31°

PERFORMANCE: (V-6, 2.8-litre)
Max speed   150 km/h (93 mph)
Power-to-weight ratio   12.2 kg/hp (26.89 lb/hp)
Fuel consumption   12–20 litres/100 km (2.63–4.39 gallons/62 miles)

How AMC reach the US ski-set, the top of the range Cherokee Chief

JEEP CJ-7

Jeep CJ-7 Renegade

The mystique of the Jeep, especially in any form resembling the early MB and CJ-2 series, has never been equalled by any other manufacturer. With the CJ-7, AMC finally produced a rationalised range of engine and accommodation options which allowed it to be as much at home in the King's Road as on the Baja 500.

MANUFACTURER: Jeep Corporation, Southfield, Michigan, USA

CONFIGURATION: 4 × 4, front-engined, open body with canvas top, hard top, wagon and van

	doors	seats	unladen weight	max load
Open body	–	4	1183 kg (2600 lb)	520 kg (1146 lb)
Hard top	2	4		
Wagon	3	6	1354 kg (2985 lb)	530 kg (1168 lb)
Van	3	2	1354 kg (2985 lb)	530 kg (1168 lb)

ENGINE:
i) 4-cylinder, 2466 cc, water-cooled petrol developing 84 hp at 3600 rpm
Torque 169 Nm at 2600 rpm
Compression ratio 8.6:1
ii) 6-cylinder, 4231 cc, water-cooled petrol developing 110 hp at 3000 rpm
Torque 277 Nm at 1800 rpm
Compression ratio 8.6:1
iii) 4-cylinder, 2369 cc, water-cooled diesel
Compression ratio 20:1

TRANSMISSION:
Manual, 4-speed or 5-speed, automatic
Type of clutch single dry plate
Number of gear ratios i) 4 forward, 1 reverse
1) 4.03:1 2) 2.37:1 3) 1.50:1 4) 1:1
Rev. 3.76:1 Final drive 3.54:1 (6-cylinder 3.31:1, 4-cylinder diesel 4.09:1)
ii) 5-speed 5 forward, 1 reverse
1) 4.03:1 2) 2.37:1 3) 1.50:1 4) 1:1 5) 0.85:1
Rev. 3.76:1 Final drive 4.09:1

CHASSIS AND SUSPENSION: Ladder frame type. Semi-elliptical leaf springs all round with telescopic shock absorbers

Fuel tank	56 litres (12.3 gallons), 76 litres (16.7 gallons) optional
Brakes	discs front, drums rear with servo
Steering	recirculating ball
Tyres	P205/75 R15
Electrical system	12V

DIMENSIONS:

Length	1.417 m (4 ft 8 in)
Width	1.659 m (5 ft 5 in)
Height	1.801 m (5 ft 11 in) (open body), 1.803 m (5 ft 11 in) (hard top) 1.834 (6 ft) (wagon & van)
Wheelbase	2.372 m (7 ft 9 in)
Track	1.417 m/1.4 m (rear) (4 ft 8 in/4 ft 7 in)
Turning radius	5.45 m (17 ft 10 in)
Ground clearance	0.21 m (8 in)
Angle of approach/departure	45°/30°

PERFORMANCE:
6-cylinder, 4.2-litre
Max speed	140 km/h (87 mph)
Power-to-weight ratio	11 kg/hp (24.25 lb/hp)
Fuel consumption	12–20 litres/100 km (2.5–4.3 gallons/62 miles)

4-cylinder, 2.46-litre
Max speed	120 km/h (75 mph)
Power-to-weight ratio	11.3 kg/hp (25 lb/hp)
Fuel consumption	11–18 litres/100 km (2.4–3.9 gallons/62 miles)

4-cylinder, 2.4-litre diesel
Max speed	100 km/h (62 mph)
Power-to-weight ratio	18.2 kg/hp (39.68 lb/hp)
Fuel consumption	9–15 litres/100 km (1.9–3.2 gallons/62 miles)

JEEP CJ-8

Jeep CJ-8 panel van

The long wheelbase CJ-8 range was launched in 1982 and shares engine, transmission and styling package options with the CJ-7 including from 1984, the new 2.5 litre 4-cylinder petrol engine. Wagon and Van models are marketed outside the USA.

MANUFACTURER: Jeep Corporation, Southfield, Michigan, USA

CONFIGURATION: 4 × 4, front-engined, open body with canvas top, station wagon, van

	doors	seats	unladen weight	max load
Open body	–	4	1220 kg (2688 lb)	274 kg (604 lb)
Hard top	2	4	1220 kg (2688 lb)	274 kg (604 lb)
Wagon	3	8	1354 kg (2985 lb)	550 kg (1212 lb)
Van	3	2	1354 kg (2985 lb)	900 kg (1984 lb)

ENGINE: i) 4-cylinder, 2466 cc, water-cooled petrol developing 84 hp at 3600 rpm
Torque 169 Nm at 2600 rpm
Compression ratio 8.6:1
ii) 6-cylinder, 4231 cc, water-cooled petrol developing 110 hp at 3000 rpm
Torque 277 Nm at 1800 rpm
Compression ratio 8.6:1
iii) 4-cylinder, 2369 cc, water-cooled diesel
Compression ratio 20:1

TRANSMISSION: Manual, 4-speed or 5-speed, automatic
Type of clutch single dry plate
Number of gear ratios i) 4 forward, 1 reverse
1) 4.03:1 2) 2.37:1 3) 1.5:1 4) 1:1
Rev. 3.76:1 Final drive 3.54:1 (6-cylinder 3.31:1, 4-cylinder diesel 4.09:1)
ii) 5 forward, 1 reverse
1) 40.3:1 2) 2.37:1 3) 1.5:1 4) 1:1 5) 0.85:1
Rev. 3.76:1 Final drive 4.09:1

CHASSIS AND SUSPENSION: Ladder frame type. Semi-elliptical leaf springs all round with telescopic shock absorbers

Fuel tank	56 litres (12.3 gallons), 76 litres (16.7 gallons) optional
Brakes	discs front, drums rear with servo
Steering	recirculating ball
Tyres	P205/75R 15
Electrical system	12V

DIMENSIONS:

Length	4.5 m (14 ft 9 in)
Width	1.659 m (5 ft 5 in)
Height	1.798 m (5 ft 11 in) (open body), 1.816 m (5 ft 11 in) (hard top) 1.834 m (6 ft) (wagon/van)
Wheelbase	2.626 m (8 ft 7 in)
Track	1.42 m/1.40 m (rear) (4 ft 8 in/4 ft 7 in)
Turning radius	5.9 m (19 ft)
Ground clearance	0.21 m (8 in)
Angle of approach/departure	45°/26.5°

Little is sacred in the US off-road scene but the results are often impressive as this bigfoot CJ-3A demonstrates

JEEP GRAND WAGONEER

Grand Wagoneer Station Wagon

The Wagoneer line goes back to the early sixties with the launch of the J100 series station wagons by Willys Motors which wrapped Detroit big car styling around the rugged four-wheel drive utility of the Jeep line.

The model featured the full time four-wheel drive system called Quadra-Trac from 1973 and, while the bodywork remained virtually the same, the Wagoneer's front end has kept pace with other Detroit renditions in chrome.

Today's Grand Wagoneer (formerly marketed as the Wagoneer Limited) is a lineal descendant offering 'traditional' styling in a big four-wheel drive package and the company bills it as the 'largest four-door wagon available in the four-wheel drive industry'.

MANUFACTURER: AMC Jeep, Toledo, Ohio, USA

CONFIGURATION: 4 × 4, front-engined, station wagon

	doors	seats	unladen weight	max load
6-cyl.	5	6	1918 kg (4229 lb)	800 kg (1764 lb)
V-8	5	6	2023 kg (4461 lb)	680 kg (1499 lb)

ENGINE:
i) 6-cylinder, 4231 cc, water-cooled petrol developing 112 hp at 3400 rpm
Torque   271 Nm at 2000 rpm
Compression ratio   8.6:1
ii) V-8, 5904 cc, water-cooled petrol developing 157 hp at 4200 rpm
Torque   346 Nm at 1400 rpm
Compression ratio   8.25:1

TRANSMISSION:
Automatic
Type of clutch   single dry plate
Number of gear ratios   3 forward, 1 reverse
1) 2.74:1   2) 1.55:1   3) 1.00:1   Rev. 2.20:1
Final drive   2.73:1   3.31:1 optional
Transfer box   2-speed   1:1/2.61:1

CHASSIS AND SUSPENSION:
Box section ladder type. Semi-elliptical leaf springs with telescopic shock absorbers front and rear

Fuel tank	77 litres (16.94 gallons)
Brakes	discs front, drums rear with servo
Steering	recirculating ball with power assist
Tyres	225/75R15
Electrical system	12V

DIMENSIONS:

Length	4.735 m (15 ft 6 in)
Width	1.901 m (6 ft 3 in)
Height	1.607 m (5 ft 3 in)
Wheelbase	2.761 m (9 ft)
Track	1.509 m/1.468 m (rear) (4 ft 11 in/4 ft 9 in)
Turning radius	5.75 m (18 ft 9 in)
Ground clearance	0.25 m (10 in)
Angle of approach/departure	39°/20°

PERFORMANCE:
6-cylinder, 4.2-litre

Max speed	130 km/h (81 mph)
Power-to-weight ratio	17.1 kg/hp (38 lb/hp)
Fuel consumption	15–21 litres/100 km (3.3–4.6 gallons/62 miles)

V-8, 5.9-litre

Max speed	160 km/h (99 mph)
Power-to-weight ratio	12.9 kg/hp (28 lb/hp)
Fuel consumption	16–23 litres/100 km (3.5–5 gallons/62 miles)

JEEP CJ-10

CJ-10

Looking like a classic CJ series Jeep that has been pulled lengthways to make a truck, the CJ10 was launched in 1982 as a full size pick-up in the Jeep mould. The CJ-10 is offered in open, hard top cab and steel top cab forms with petrol or diesel engines in base, custom and deluxe option packages. The front and styling may offend the purists but shades of the M38 are still there.

MANUFACTURER:	AMC Jeep CJ-10			
CONFIGURATION:	4 × 4, front-engined, open body pick-up, hard top cab			
	doors	**seats**	**unladen weight**	**max load**
	2	2	1540 kg (3396 lb)	1315 kg (2899 lb)

ENGINE:	i) 6-cylinder, 4231 cc, water-cooled petrol ii) 6-cylinder, 3250 cc, water-cooled diesel
TRANSMISSION:	Manual or automatic (petrol model only) Type of clutch — single dry plate Number of gear ratios — 4 forward, 1 reverse 1) 4.03:1 2) 2.37:1 3) 1.5:1 4) 1:1 Rev. 3.76:1 Final drive 4.09:1 Transfer box — 2-speed 1:1/2.61:1
CHASSIS AND SUSPENSION:	Ladder frame. Semi-elliptical leaf springs all round
	Fuel tank — 77 litres (16.9 gallons) Brakes — discs front, drums rear with servo Steering — recirculating ball Tyres — 7.50 × 16 Electrical system — 12V
DIMENSIONS:	Length — 4.85 m (15 ft 11 in) Width — 1.73 m (5 ft 7 in) Height — 1.83 m (6 ft) Wheelbase — 3.04 m (10 ft) Track — 1.54 m/1.48 m (5 ft/4 ft 10 in) Turning radius — 6.55 m (21 ft 6 in) Ground clearance — 0.23 m (8 in)

JEEP J-10, JEEP J-20 TRUCK

The J-10/J-20 truck series shares the front end sheet metal and much of the mechanics of the Wagoneer line. Standard suspension on the J-20 allows payloads up to 1553 kg with an optional heavy duty suspension accommodating up to 1898 kg (4185 lb).

Both models are offered with six-cylinder 4.2 litre or V-8 5.9 litre engines, four-speed manual or optional automatic transmission on the V-8 plus 'Selec-Trac' optional 4 × 2 or 4 × 2 and on road four-wheel drive. Both truck lines are available with Pioneer or Laredo styling packages.

MANUFACTURER:	AMC Jeep, Toledo, Ohio, USA			
CONFIGURATION:	4 × 4, front-engined pick-up with steel top cab on two wheelbases			
	doors	**seats**	**unladen weight**	**max load**
J-10 Swb	2	2	1690 kg (3726 lb)	1020 kg (2249 lb)
J-10 Lwb	2	2	1730 kg (3814 lb)	980 kg (2160 lb)
J-20 V-8	2	2	1963 kg (4328 lb)	1487 kg (3279 lb)

ENGINE:	i) 6-cylinder, 4231 cc, water-cooled petrol ii) V-8, 5904 cc, water-cooled petrol
TRANSMISSION:	4-speed manual or 3-speed automatic selectable 4 × 2 or 4 × 4 Type of clutch — single dry plate Number of gear ratios — 4 forward, 1 reverse Transfer box — 2-speed
CHASSIS AND SUSPENSION:	Box section ladder type. Semi-elliptical leaf springs all round
	Fuel tank — 68.9 (15.2 gallons) Brakes — discs front, drums rear with servo Steering — recirculating ball Tyres — P225/75R 15 Electrical system — 12V
DIMENSIONS:	**J-10 swb** Length — 4.928 m (16 ft 2 in) Width — 2 m (6 ft 6 in) Height — 1.753 m (5 ft 8 in) Wheelbase — 3.018 m (9 ft 11 in) Track — 1.608/1.621 m (rear) (5 ft 3 in/5 ft 4 in) Turning radius — 20.3 m (66 ft 7 in) Ground clearance — 0.256 m (10 in) Angle of approach/departure — 45°/26° **J-10 lwb** Length — 5.232 m (17 ft 2 in) Width — 2 m (6 ft 6 in) Height — 1.765 m (5 ft 9 in) Wheelbase — 3.322 m (10 ft 11 in) Track — 1.608 m/1.621 m (rear) (5 ft 3 in/5 ft 4 in) Turning radius — 22.5 m (73 ft 10 in) **J-20** Length — 5.232 m (17 ft 2 in) Width — 2 m (6 ft 6 in) Height — 1.778 m (5 ft 10 in) Wheelbase — 3.322 m (10 ft 11 in) Track — 1.626 m/1.661 m (rear) (5 ft 5 in/5 ft 6 in) Turning radius — 22.5 m (73 ft 10 in) Angle of approach/departure — 45°/27°

Jeep J-20 truck

Without the financial muscle of the US big three, American Motors Jeep Corporation relies rather on quality and tradition to continue to sell its wares rather than re-tooling and spurious 'new' models. The production of the Jeep line is far more labour intensive than is standard in Detroit but if it costs more, the pay off is in reliability and build quality. Things have changed since 1945 however including a brand new cataphoretic rust-proofing process introduced at the Toledo, Ohio plant.

Engines come from the company's own engine foundry except for the 2.0 litre Renault engines which to begin with were shipped in and re-exported to the European market, one result of the AMC-Renault technical and marketing tie-up. From 1984 assembly of complete vehicles from knocked down components began in France.

This sequence shows, (right) CJ-7s in the paint shop, (far right) checking the phosphate coatings on CJ-7 major body components, (far right below) Jeep Cherokee Chiefs in the final assembly shop.

Finished Jeeps are test driven around the factory's perimeter tracks and random vehicles are batch tested for quality control. The longevity of the Jeep, with many wartime veterans still surviving, is its own example

WILLYS M-38, M38A1

Just before the end of the Pacific war, Willys Overland produced the first Jeeps for the civilian market, closely followed in August 1945 by a redesigned model, the CJ-2A or 'Universal Jeep'. The main changes were a redesigned front end with seven vertical slats in the radiator instead of the wartime Model MB's nine sealed beam headlights, a tailgate and side rear mounting for the spare wheel, plus steering column-mounted gearshift. In 1949 this vehicle was supplanted by the CJ-3A with the gearshift back on the floor, a single-piece windscreen and other detail changes.

With the commitment to the Korean War, the US Army suddenly needed to replace its remaining Second World War veterans and ordered a military version of the CJ-3A as the 'Truck, Utility, quarter-ton 4 × 4 M38' (Willys Overland Model MC). The M38 differed from the standard civilian vehicles in having a deep fording kit, 24-volt electrics, and other military fittings such as towing eyes and black-out lighting.

The M38 was in production from 1950 to 1952 when it in turn was replaced by the M38A1 (Willys Model MC), distinctly different in appearance to the M38. The more bulbous front end is distinguished by headlights cutting out into the grille, integral front wings, and a longer wheelbase (81 inches compared to 80). The power unit was the 72 hp F-head (inlet over exhaust valves) engine, and the front and restyling the bigger engine occasioned is still there twenty-five years later in Jeep Corporation's civilian CJ line of products.

The M38A1 was manufactured for the US Army from 1952 to 1962 when it was replaced by the M151 series and, although no longer in US Army service, large numbers still serve with armed forces around the world. Assembly also took place in Canada by Ford (M38A-CDN) and by Ford of Brazil (Ford U-50). The Nederlanse Kaiser Frazer-Fabriekene, and later Kemeper & Van Twist built the vehicle in the Netherlands for the Dutch Army and many of these vehicles came on the civilian market in Europe in the early 1980s.

The M38A1 is entirely conventional in layout with a full floating single reduction front axle fitted with a conventional differential with hypoid drive gears. The rear axle is a semi-floating single reduction type with the same differential specification.

The two-part windscreen folds forward and the canvas top collapses with folding bows at the rear of the vehicle.

Both the M38 and M38A1 can be fitted with a front-mounted winch.

VARIANTS

M38A1C. Weapons platform for 105 mm recoilless rifle. Split windscreen to accommodate barrel and no rear seat. Spare wheel mounted on right side rather than rear as on standard M38A1.

M170. Truck, ambulance quarter-ton 4 × 4 M170 Front Line, long wheelbase version of M38A1 able to carry three stretcher patients or six seated. Internal spare wheel stowage plus interior crash pads and lighting.

MANUFACTURER:	Jeep Corporation, Detroit, Michigan, USA			
CONFIGURATION:	4 × 4, front-engined, open body with canvas top and side screens			
		doors	seats	unladen weight	max load
	M38	–	1 + 3	1247 kg (2749 lb)	544 kg (1199 lb)
	M38A1	–	1 + 3	1209 kg (2665 lb)	544 kg (1199 lb)
	M170	–	1 + 1	1344 kg (2963 lb)	–
ENGINE:	(M38A1) Willys 4-cylinder, water-cooled petrol developing 72 hp at 4000 rpm			
TRANSMISSION:	Manual			
	Type of clutch	single dry plate		
	Number of gear ratios	4 forward, 1 reverse		
	Transfer box	2-speed		
CHASSIS AND SUSPENSION:	Separate chassis and all steel body. Semi-elliptical springs front and rear with hydraulic telescopic shock absorbers			
	Fuel tank	64.3 litres (14.14 gallons)		
	Steering	recirculating ball		
	Tyres	7.00 × 16		
	Electrical system	24V		
DIMENSIONS:	Length	3.517 m (11 ft 6 in)		
	Width	1.539 m (5 ft 1 in)		
	Height	1.85 m (6 ft 1 in)		
	Wheelbase	2.057 m (6 ft 9 in)		
	Track	1.247 m (4 ft 1 in)		
	Turning radius	5.892 m (19 ft)		
	Ground clearance	0.234 m (9 in)		
	Fording	0.939 m (3 ft 1 in)		
	Gradient	69%		
	Angle of approach/departure	55°/35°		
PERFORMANCE:	Max speed	88 km/h (55 mph)		

CANADIAN JEEPS

In 1952 the Ford Motor Company of Canada began a production run of the Willys MC, standardised as the M38 in US Army service and as the M38CDN by the Canadians. The vehicle was itself supplanted in production by a Canadian-built M38A1 (the Willys MD, the military version of the CJ-5) which had the F-head engine (inlet over exhaust) and the more rotund bonnet styling of its US-built counterpart. Leyland Motors of Canada produced ambulance and wireless version conversion kits while there were also light repair versions, weapons carriers and vehicles fitted with front-mounted winches.

To replace its ageing fleet of 4 × 4 light vehicles, the Canadian government has contracted with Bombardier Incorporated to supply a Canadian-built version of the Volkswagen Iltis 500 kg (1102 lb) light vehicle being manufactured for the West German Army as a replacement for their 1950s-generation Auto-Union 'Munga' light vehicles (see page 148).

EGYPTIAN JEEPS

After the 1956 fighting, the Egyptian armed forces began to replace the ragbag of surplus US and British military vehicles with which they were equipped, with Soviet supplied types including large quantities of GAZ-69 field cars and UAZ 450 series four-wheel drive light trucks. The GAZ-69 is also deployed by the Egyptian Army as a launch vehicle for Snapper anti-tank missiles.

In 1977 following the vicissitudes of Middle East diplomacy, the Egyptian government concluded an agreement with AMC to build the CJ-6 Jeep under licence for military and civil use and for export.

The vehicle is the basic CJ-6 with minimum adaptation, available in open form or with a glass fibre cab. The Egyptian Army has modified the vehicle as a launcher for the SA-7 Grail surface-to-air missile and for the British Swingfire anti-tank missile.

Egyptian built CJ-6 firing Swingfire missile

INDIAN JEEPS

Willys Overland reached a licence agreement with the old-established Indian engineering firm of Mahindra and Mahindra Ltd of Bombay for the licence production of Jeeps beginning with the CJ-3A. The CJ-4 was produced only in India and was a lengthened version of the CJ-3B on a wheelbase of 91 inches instead of 80. There was also a

4×2 model and both were available with enclosed bodywork, marketed as the Wagonette.

The Indian Army uses quantities of these vehicles in command and communication roles and as weapons platforms. Mahindra also supplied knocked down vehicles for final assembly in Iran.

Indian Army CJ-4

JEEPS IN MILITARY SERVICE, M606, M606A1, M606A2, M606A3, M170

The standard light vehicle of the US armed forces since the mid-1960s has been the M151, originally designed by Ford and latterly produced by AM General, successor company to the original Willys Overland. The Ford vehicle confusingly owes little to 'Jeep' lineage other than in overall configuration while, since the phasing out of the last M38A1, no pure bred 'Jeeps' as such serve with the US armed forces.

However, large numbers of Jeeps proper serve with many armies around the world often supplied under US Military Assistance Programs (MAP) or built under licence by national manufacturers which are described separately below.

M606/CJ-3B

The civilian CJ-3B first appeared in 1952 just prior to the takeover of Willys Overland by Henry J. Kaiser Industries in March 1953. The vehicle is immediately distinguishable from its predecessor, the CJ-3A (M38 in US Army service, Willys Model MC), by the higher bonnet line and deeper seven-slatted radiator grille, necessitated by the F-Head 'hurricane' engine, which gives the vehicle a far boxier appearance than the wartime vehicle and its immediate late 1940s successors the CJ-2A and CJ-3A.

The M606 has been widely exported under MAP schemes and also manufactured by a large number of licencees including Hotchkiss-Brandt of France, VIASA in Spain and Mitsubishi in Japan.

M606A2 (CJ-5)

Again supplied under MAP or licence-built locally, the M606A2 was based on the CJ-5 introduced in 1952, itself a civilianised version of the M38A1. The M606A3 was the CJ-5 fitted as a communications vehicle.

CJ-6

A long wheelbase (101-inch) variant of CJ-5 in production from 1955 with a payload capacity of 1564 lb, the CJ-6 has been adapted as a military vehicle by several armed forces.

The US Army's M170 front line ambulance was based on this vehicle.

The CJ-6, although no longer in US production, is manufactured under licence in Egypt. The CJ-5 and CJ-6 were manufactured under licence by Matmar Industries of Haifa until the late 1970s and serve with the Israeli Army.

Jeep Corporation, in addition to those mentioned above, has main assembly plants and licencees in Australia, Bangladesh, Egypt, India (Mahindra and Mahindra of Bombay q.v.), Indonesia, Israel (Matmar, now shut down), France (in partnership with Renault q.v.), Kenya, South Africa, Korea, Mexico, Morocco, Pakistan, the Philippines, Portugal (by Bravia q.v.), Spain (by VIASA), Sri Lanka, Taiwan, Thailand and Venezuela. The A38A1 was manufactured by Nekaf in the Netherlands and by Ford of Canada.

In 1983 AMC reached a production agreement with the Chinese Beijing Automotive works establishing the Beijing Jeep Corporation to manufacture Jeeps in China for export within the Far East and to Japan. Production initially would begin with the existing BJ-212 powered by AMC's new four-cylinder, 2.5-litre engine before moving on to licence manufacture of complete Jeep models. The BJ-212 serves widely with the Chinese armed forces.

Military versions of the CJ range are standardised outside the USA as the AM-7 (CJ-7), AM-8 (CJ-8) and AM-10 (CJ-10) (q.v. under civil Jeeps). The options available on the civil vehicles are available on their military counterparts including four- and five-speed gearboxes, automatic transmission, selectable four-wheel drive, diesel or petrol engines, plastic or metal hard tops, hot or cold extreme climate conditioning, various seating arrangements and heavy duty suspension.

The militarised versions feature heavy duty air cleaners, chassis reinforcements, heavy duty shock absorbers and battery clamp. All models are fitted with a night blackout lighting system plus towing hooks and eyes.

LADA NIVA VAZ-2121

Lada Niva, Soviet bridgehead in the West's growing off-road market

Built at the Togliattigrad plant in the Soviet Union the Niva displays typical Russian ruggedness with a fairly high level of sophistication, coil springs all round, and considerable creature comfort. It has consistently performed well in rallies, winning the Egyptian Rally of the Pharoahs and finishing second in the Paris–Dakar two years running. The Niva has permanent four-wheel drive with a two-speed transfer box and lockable differential.

A factory built right hand drive model for the British market was introduced in 1983 and an open top 'cabrio' in 1984.

TRANSMISSION:
Manual
Number of gear ratios 4 forward, 1 reverse
1) 3.24:1 2) 1.99:1 3) 1.29:1 4) 1:1
Rev. 3.34:1 Final drive 4.3:1
Transfer box 2-speed 1.2:1/2.135:1

CHASSIS AND SUSPENSION:
Unitary construction. Independent front suspension by coil springs, rear rigid axle with coil springs, telescopic double-acting hydraulic shock absorbers all round

Fuel tank	45 litres (9.89 gallons)
Brakes	discs front, drums rear with vacuum assist
Steering	worm and roller
Tyres	6.95 ×16
Electrical system	12V

DIMENSIONS:

Length	3.72 m (12 ft 2 in)
Width	1.68 m (5 ft 6 in)
Height	1.64 m (5 ft 4 in)
Wheelbase	2.2 m (7 ft 3 in)
Track	1.43 m/1.4 m (rear) (4 ft 8 in/4 ft 7 in)
Turning radius	5.8 m (19 ft)
Ground clearance	0.22 m (9 in)
Gradient	58%

MANUFACTURER: Volzhsky Automobilny Zavod, Togliattigrad, Soviet Union

CONFIGURATION: 4 ×4, front-engined, station wagon

	doors	seats	unladen weight	max load
VAZ-2121	3	4–5	1150 kg (2535 lb)	840 kg (1852 lb)

ENGINE:
4-cylinder, 1569 cc, water-cooled petrol developing 80 hp at 4500 rpm

Torque	122 Nm at 3200 rpm
Compression ratio	8.5:1

PERFORMANCE:

Max speed	132 km/h (82 mph)
Power-to-weight ratio	14.7 kg/hp (32.4 lb/hp)
Fuel consumption	10.4–13.7 litres/100 km (2.29–3.01 gallons/62 miles)

LAMBORGHINI LMA

The Italian supercar manufacturer Lamborghini began a flirtation with four-wheel drive in 1977 and have exhibited various prototypes but have yet to get a vehicle into series production.

The V-8 engined 'Cheetah' was built in 1977 the big engine delivering tremendous power and acceleration – too much indeed for the US Army who wrecked it under test.

A new prototype was constructed first with a 5.9-litre AMC engine (LM 002), then a 4.8-litre Lamborghini V-12 (LM 002/4) with a four-speed manual box. The LMA was a further rebuild with the engine repositioned in the front offered either with the 4.8-litre V-12 or a massive 7-litre unit. Lamborghini intend selling the LMA to military and non-military customers at a price 'around that of a Countach'.

MANUFACTURER:	Lamborghini SpA, Bologna, Italy

CONFIGURATION:	4 ×4, front-engined, utility saloon			
		doors	seats	unladen weight
	LMA	4	4	2600 kg (5732 lb)

ENGINE:	V-12, 4754 cc, water-cooled petrol developing 332 hp at 6000 rpm	
	Torque	427 Nm at 4500 rpm
	Compression ratio	9:1

TRANSMISSION:	Manual	
	Type of clutch	single dry plate
	Number of gear ratios	5 forward, 1 reverse
	1) 2.99:1 2) 1.9:1 3) 1.33:1 4) 1:1 5) 0.89:1	
	Rev. 2.7:1 Final drive 4.125:1	
	Transfer box	2-speed

CHASSIS AND SUSPENSION:	Tubular construction with GRP body. Independent front suspension with coil springs, independent rear suspension with coil springs, telescopic shock absorbers all round	
	Fuel tank	280 litres (61.6 gallons)
	Brakes	dual circuit discs front and rear, servo
	Steering	rack and pinion, servo
	Tyres	14 ×16
	Electrical system	12V

DIMENSIONS:	LMA	
	Length	4.79 m (15 ft 7 in)
	Width	2 m (6 ft 6 in)
	Height	1.85 m (6 ft)
	Wheelbase	2.95 m (9 ft 7 in)
	Track	1.615 m (5 ft 3 in)

PERFORMANCE:	Max speed	188 km/h (116 mph)
	Power-to-weight ratio	7.8 kg/hp (17 lb/hp)
	Fuel consumption	20 litres/100 km (4.4 gallons/62 miles)

LAMBORGHINI LM004

MANUFACTURER:	Lamborghini SpA, Bologna, Italy

CONFIGURATION:	4 ×4, front-engined, utility saloon			
		doors	seats	unladen weight
	LM004	4	4	2600 kg (5732 lb)

ENGINE:	V-12, 7000 cc, water-cooled petrol developing 420 hp at 5400 rpm	
	Torque	589 Nm at 3500 rpm

TRANSMISSION:	Manual	
	Type of clutch	single dry plate
	Number of gear ratios	5 forward, 1 reverse
	1) 2.422:1 2) 1.792:1 3) 1.304:1 4) 1:1	
	5) 0.746:1 Rev. 2.867:1	

CHASSIS AND SUSPENSION:	Fuel tank	320 litres (17.4 gallons)
	Brakes	discs at front, drums rear
	Tyres	325/65VR ×17
	Electrical system	12V

DIMENSIONS:	Length	4.9 m (16 ft 1 in)
	Width	2 m (6 ft 6 in)
	Height	1.85 m (6 ft 1 in)
	Wheelbase	3 m (9 ft 10 in)
	Track	1.61 m (5 ft 4 in)
	Turning radius	6.1 m (20 ft)
	Ground clearance	0.29 m (1 ft)

PERFORMANCE:	Max speed	205 km/h (127 mph)
	Power-to-weight ratio	6.4 kg/hp (14 lb/hp)

CIVIL LAND ROVERS

Show the uninitiated a modern off-road vehicle and they'll either call it a 'Jeep' or a Land-Rover. But being early in the field brings penalties. The market leadership of the British vehicle was taken for granted for years and while it technically stagnated, newer rivals pushed in on its markets, civil and military. New investment and new vehicles, however, are set to redress the balance in the eighties. The Land-Rover first saw the light of day at the Amsterdam Motor Show in April 1948, in the years of postwar austerity when the British motor industry was pushing desperately for exports and unveiling its first truly new postwar product in the attempt to get them. The Land-Rover was a product of both imperatives – austerity and the export drive. The Rover company needed something to get its export sales up and thus its government-controlled steel allocation up into the bargain. The company decided to build an all-purpose, cross-country field car and design work began by fitting a war surplus Willys with Rover engine and gearbox using Willys suspension components. In deference to agricultural practice, the steering wheel was mounted centrally as on a tractor.

The first production model was, however, a brand new vehicle with the characteristic Land-Rover configuration that would still be identifiable in the company's products thirty-five years later. The body made extensive use of aluminium on a very strong box girder chassis giving both toughness and durability plus a low centre of gravity and good power-to-weight ratio, ideal factors for off-road performance. The first model had an 80-inch wheelbase and the contemporary four-cylinder, F-head, 1595 cc petrol engine from the Rover 60 P3 car. The first models were simple open pick-up types with a canvas hood but the first enclosed estate models were offered a few months after quantity production began at the Solihull factory in July 1948.

The Series I Land-Rover began its military career with the British Army in 1949 and had its first test in the Korean War where the tough going showed up several shortcomings and development paths. The Land-Rover went on to become the British Army's standard quarter-ton 4×4 light vehicle, pushing aside the Austin Champ, as well as serving with over 140 military services worldwide. The development of military Land-Rovers is covered in a later entry.

In 1952 the 1.6-litre engine was replaced by a 2-litre petrol engine and, in 1954, the original 80-inch wheelbase was supplanted by an 86-inch wheelbase model. In August 1953 a long wheelbase version of the open pick-up was introduced with a 107-inch wheelbase and a 750 kg (1654 lb) cargo capacity. A ten-seat hard top station wagon on this wheelbase was introduced in November 1955.

The Series I Land-Rovers went through another change in June 1956. The short wheelbase was increased to 88 inches while the 107-inch models were run on until November 1958. In 1957 a 2-litre diesel engine option was offered.

In February 1958 the Series II was introduced in both 88-inch and, briefly, 107-inch wheelbases with a 2.25-litre petrol engine or diesel, as an option. The Series II

vehicles are externally distinguishable by sills below the doors and an external fuel filler cap while there were several mechanical changes under the skin. In March 1958 a new Series II pick-up was introduced on a 109-inch wheelbase and a 12-seater station wagon on this wheelbase was introduced in November that year when production of 107-inch wheelbase vehicles was discontinued.

The Series IIA introduced in September 1961 had minor modifications with a 2.25-litre diesel or petrol engine. The Series II vehicles continued in production through the 1960s commanding a large export and military market but meanwhile competitors, particularly the Japanese, were beginning to make inroads while technically the British vehicle began to grow whiskery. Meanwhile from early 1967 a 2.6-litre petrol engine was offered on the long wheelbase model.

The Land-Rover design team had something completely new up their sleeve however in the Range Rover, set to break on the world's automotive market in 1970.

Meanwhile, from early 1967, a 2.6-litre petrol engine was offered on the long wheelbase model and Land-Rover in 1966 developed the prototype 564 kg air-portable military vehicle in consort with the UK Military Vehicle Experimental Establishment.

Vehicle construction regulations in the Benelux market took the headlights to the front wings in 1968, standardised on all vehicles from 1969. In October 1971 the Series III vehicles were introduced with a new, somewhat fussy grille, redesigned instrument panel and facia, all syncromesh gearbox and many detailed improvements. The 3.5-litre V-8 petrol engine from the Range Rover was offered on the Series III from 1980.

In March 1983 Land-Rover launched the most significant development of the basic vehicle since its debut after a period of capital investment and restructuring of the manufacturing operation centred at Solihull. The new vehicle, called the Land-Rover One Ten, combined the Land-Rover's utility with the Range Rover's chassis and long travel suspension system with coil springs at front and rear on a 110-inch wheelbase. The vehicle is externally distinguished by a new, one-piece windscreen and injection-moulded black plastic radiator grille and lamp surrounds. Wheel arch extensions made of glass-reinforced polyurethane secured by frangible nylon pegs which will give way in a crash emphasise the vehicle's wide track stance.

In June 1984 the One Ten's stablemate was announced, the Land-Rover Ninety, offering the same kind of engineering on a 90-inch wheelbase. Both new vehicles have redesigned interiors and increased passenger comfort with wind-up windows, saloon car type facia, adjustable seats, rear window wash/wipe and other options listed below. The 'County' model is offered on both wheelbases with carpeting throughout, head restraints, cloth seats, tinted glass and radio speakers, competing directly for the big estate car market. Its off-road performance perhaps is an afterthought for the *rus in urbe* four-wheel drive fanciers but it's certainly at home at the point-to-point with a Fortnum's hamper as the optional extra.

LAND ROVER 90

Land Rover 90 in top of the range 'County' trim

MANUFACTURER: Land-Rover, Solihull, England

CONFIGURATION: 4×4, front-engined, open body with canvas top, pick-up, station wagon or hard top, various special bodies

	doors	seats	unladen weight	max load
Soft top	2	2–7	1487 kg (3278 lb)	913 kg (2013 lb)
Pick-up	2	2–7	1516 kg (3342 lb)	884 kg (1949 lb)
Hard top	3	2–7	1529 kg (3371 lb)	871 kg (1920 lb)
Station wagon	3	6–7	1571 kg (3463 lb)	829 kg (1828 lb)
High load suspension				
Soft top			1514 kg (3338 lb)	1036 kg (2284 lb)
Pick-up			1543 kg (3401 lb)	1007 kg (2220 lb)
Hard top			1556 kg (3430 lb)	994 kg (2191 lb)
Station wagon			1598 kg (3523 lb)	952 kg (2099 lb)

(diesel unladen weight c. 37 kg heavier)

ENGINE: i) 4-cylinder, 2286 cc, water-cooled petrol developing 74 hp at 4000 rpm
Torque   163 Nm at 2000 rpm
Compression ratio   8:1
ii) 4-cylinder, 2495 cc, water-cooled diesel developing 67 hp at 4000 rpm
Torque   114 Nm at 1800 rpm
Compression ratio   21:1

TRANSMISSION: Manual, permanent 4×4, lockable central differential
Type of clutch   single dry plate
Number of gear ratios   5 forward, 1 reverse
1) 3.585:1   2) 2.301:1   3) 1.507:1   4) 1:1
5) 0.831:1   Rev. 3.3701:1   Final drive 3.54:1
Transfer box   2-speed   1.411:1/3.32:1

CHASSIS AND SUSPENSION: Box section ladder type, aluminium body, live beam axles front and rear with coil springs and double-acting hydraulic shock absorbers (dual rate rear coil springs on high load suspension)

Fuel tank	54.5 litres (11.99 gallons)
Brakes	discs front, drums rear, power assist
Steering	worm and roller, power assist optional
Tyres	6.00 × 16
Electrical system	12V

DIMENSIONS:

Soft top
Length	3.72 m (12 ft 2 in)
Width	1.79 m (5 ft 10 in)
Height	1.965 m (6 ft 5 in)
Height (2550 kg)	2 m (6 ft 7 in)
Wheelbase	2.36 m (7 ft 9 in)
Track	1.486 m (4 ft 10 in)
Turning radius	5.75 m (19 ft)
Ground clearance	1.98 m–2.29 m (6 ft 6 in–7 ft 6 in) according to suspension
Fording	0.5 m (1 ft 8 in)
Gradient	100%
Angle of approach/departure	47°/48°

Pick-up
Length	3.72 m (12 ft 2 in)
Width	1.79 m (5 ft 10 in)
Height	1.963 m (6 ft 5 in)
Height (2550 kg)	1.993 m (6 ft 6 in)

Hard top
Length	3.883 m (12 ft 9 in)
Width	1.79 m (5 ft 10 in)
Height	1.972 m (6 ft 6 in)
Height (2550 kg)	1.997 m (6 ft 7 in)

Station wagon
Length	3.883 m (12 ft 9 in)
Width	1.79 m (5 ft 10 in)
Height	1.963 m (6 ft 5 in)
Height (2550 kg)	1.989 m (6 ft 6 in)

The 90 shows extensive restyling within the Land Rover tradition

The Range Rover, much copied but still the world's standard in luxury four wheel drive

LAND ROVER 110

MANUFACTURER:	Land-Rover, Solihull, England		
CONFIGURATION:	4 × 4, front-engined open body with canvas top, pick-up, station wagon, hard top, crew cab, various special bodies		

	doors	seats	unladen weight	max load
Soft top (petrol)	2	2–11	1588 kg (3500 lb)	1352 kg (2980 lb)
Pick-up (3.5 petrol)	2	2–11	1574 kg (3470 lb)	1376 kg (3033 lb)
Hard top (2.5 diesel)	3	2–11	1663 kg (3666 lb)	1287 kg (2837 lb)
Station wagon (2.3 petrol)	5	9–12	1762 kg (3885 lb)	1188 kg (2619 lb)
High capacity pick-up (2.3 petrol)	2	2–3	1668 kg (3677 lb)	1262 kg (2782 lb)

ENGINE:	i) 4-cylinder, 2286 cc, water-cooled petrol developing 74 hp at 4000 rpm
	Torque 163 Nm at 2000 rpm
	Compression ratio 8:1
TRANSMISSION:	Manual, permanent 4 × 4, lockable central differential
	Type of clutch single dry plate
	Number of gear ratios 5 forward, 1 reverse
	1) 3.585:1 2) 2.301:1 3) 1.507:1 4) 1:1
	5) 0.831:1 Rev. 3.701:1 Final drive 3.54:1
ENGINE:	ii) 4-cylinder, 2495 cc, water-cooled diesel developing 67 hp at 4000 rpm
	Torque 155 Nm at 1800 rpm
	Compression ratio 21:1
TRANSMISSION:	As 2.3-litre petrol
ENGINE:	iii) V-8, 3528 cc, water-cooled petrol developing 85 hp at 4000 rpm
	Torque 251 Nm at 2500 rpm
	Compression ratio: 8.13:1
TRANSMISSION:	Manual, permanent 4 × 4, lockable central differential
	Number of gear ratios 4 forward, 1 reverse
	1) 4.069:1 2) 2.448:1 3) 1.505:1 4) 1:1
	Rev. 3.664:1 Final drive 3.54:1

CHASSIS AND SUSPENSION:	Box section ladder type. Aluminium body. Live beam axles front and rear with coil springs and double-acting shock absorbers	
	Fuel tank	80 litres (17.59 gallons)
	Brakes	discs front, drums rear, power assist
	Steering	worm and roller, power assist optional
	Tyres	7.50 × 16
	Electrical system	12V

DIMENSIONS:	Soft top	
	Length	4.438 m (14 ft 7 in)
	Width	1.79 m (5 ft 10 in)
	Height	2.035 m (6 ft 8 in)
	Wheelbase	2.794 m (9 ft 2 in)
	Track	1.486 m (4 ft 10 in)
	Turning radius	6.4 m (21 ft)
	Ground clearance	0.215 m (8 in)
	Fording	0.5 m (1 ft 8 in)
	Gradient	100%
	Angle of approach/departure	50°/35°
	Pick-up	
	Length	4.438 m (14 ft 7 in)
	Hard top	
	Length	4.605 m (15 ft 1 in)
	Station wagon	
	Length	4.605 m (15 ft 1 in)

Origin of a species – the prototype Land Rover c1947, in fact a much modified Willys Jeep with Rover drive train

Since its inception the Land Rover has been the platform for a huge range of civil and military variants. The Land Rover 1000 kg truck with forward control (left with RAF Chinook helicopters) was in production for the British Army 1975–76 but was not offered for commercial sale. A typical role is towing the 105mm Light Gun. Among many alternative special bodies on standard and modified six-wheel chassis are fire engine (top) and water tanker bottom. The Range Rover has similarly been adapted to a variety of roles including crash tender for the RAF (centre)

LAND ROVER Mk III, 88-inch wheelbase

MANUFACTURER:	Land-Rover, Solihull, England

CONFIGURATION: 4 × 4, front-engined, open body with canvas top, pick-up, station wagon

	doors	seats	unladen weight	max load
Open body	2	3–7	1430 kg (3153 lb)	690 kg (1521 lb)

ENGINE:
i) 4-cylinder, water-cooled diesel, developing 61 bhp at 4000 rpm
ii) 4-cylinder, water-cooled petrol, developing 69 bhp at 4000 rpm

TRANSMISSION:
Manual
Type of clutch — single dry plate
Number of gear ratios — 4 forward, 1 reverse
Transfer box — 2-speed

CHASSIS AND SUSPENSION: Channel section ladder type, aluminium body. Semi-elliptical springs all round with double-acting telescopic shock absorbers

Fuel tank	45 litres (9.89 gallons)
Brakes	drums all round
Steering	recirculating ball
Tyres	7.50 × 16
Electrical system	12V (24V optional)

DIMENSIONS:

Length	3.65 m (12 ft)
Width	1.68 m (5 ft 6 in)
Height	1.97 m (6 ft 5 in)
Wheelbase	2.23 m (7 ft 4 in)
Track	1.33 m (4 ft 4 in)
Turning radius	5.79 m (19 ft)
Ground clearance	0.2 m (8 in)
Angle of approach/departure	46°/30°

PERFORMANCE:	Max speed	105 km/h (65 mph)

LAND ROVER 564 Kg AIR PORTABLE LIGHT VEHICLE

Developed by Land-Rover in conjunction with MVRE as a purpose-designed, air-portable light vehicle for the British armed services in the mid-sixties, the vehicle is now the standard four-wheel drive in its class. The engine, running gear, axles, brakes and suspension are derived from the Mark III short wheelbase civilian vehicle, modified to meet military specifications.

The basic vehicle has 12-volt electrics but an FFR (fitted for radio) version is available with 24-volt electrics.

Various variants are in service having been developed to meet specific military requirements from overseas customers. The Dutch army vehicle for example has a diesel engine (56 bhp) and 24-volt electrics as standard.

MANUFACTURER:	Land-Rover, Solihull, England

CONFIGURATION: 4 × 4, front-engined, open body with canvas hood

doors	seats	unladen weight	max load
2	1 + 2 (cab)	1386 kg (3056 lb)	564 kg (1243 lb)

ENGINE:
i) 4-cylinder, 2286 cc, water-cooled petrol, developing 70 bhp at 4000 rpm
ii) 4-cylinder, 2286 cc, water-cooled diesel, developing 60 bhp at 4000 rpm

TRANSMISSION:
Manual
Type of clutch — single dry plate
Number of gear ratios — 4 forward, 1 reverse
Transfer box — 2-speed

CHASSIS AND SUSPENSION: Box section ladder type with aluminium bodywork. Semi-elliptical leaf springs all round with hydraulic shock absorbers

Fuel tank	90 litres (19.79 gallons)
Brakes	drums all round, power assist
Steering	recirculating ball
Tyres	6.50 × 16
Electrical system	12V

DIMENSIONS:

Length	3.65 m (12 ft)
Width	1.52 m (5 ft)
Height	1.95 m (6 ft 5 in)
Wheelbase	2.23 m (7 ft 4 in)
Track	1.31 m (4 ft 3 in)
Turning radius	6.4 m (21 ft)
Ground clearance	0.21 m (8 in)
Fording	0.5 m (1 ft 8 in) (with kit)
Gradient	115%
Angle of approach/departure	49°/36°

PERFORMANCE:	Max speed	105 km/h (65 mph)

RANGE ROVER

When the Range Rover was unveiled in June 1970 it really did break new automotive ground. It was not so much from the point of view of technical innovation but in the combination of features and the new market slot the vehicle was aimed at. The style it brought to four-wheel drive has been widely copied since but the Range Rover's combination of form and function remains out in front.

There had been big four-wheel drive estates before such as the Jeep Wagoneer and Toyota Land Cruiser but never with the style, the comfort and purpose-designed engineering of the Range Rover. It combined the luxuries of a big station wagon with the engineering of a heavy duty utility vehicle. It was at home wallowing in the mud, in the member's car park at the polo club or cruising at high speed on the highway.

Based on a rugged steel chassis, the vehicle's rubber-mounted steel body frame is clad in aluminium panels. Power comes from a big, V-8, light alloy engine developing 125 bhp driving through a four-speed gearbox (on the original vehicle) with a two-speed transfer case. Four-wheel drive is permanent with a lockable central differential for maximum traction.

Beam axles with long travel coil springs all round and disc brakes give optimum comfort and handling at speed and surefootedness off the road.

The Range Rover benefited from Land-Rover's new investment at the outset of the 1980s and has been considerably refined and improved. Creature comforts within have been refined and the top of the range 'Vogue' model, based on the four-door introduced in 1981, features electrically-operated windows and door mirrors and other luxury details.

Range Rover 6 × 6, modification by Scottorn Trailers

There are more significant changes under the skin, however, including Lucas electronic ignition and a new five-speed manual transmission introduced in 1983.

MANUFACTURER:	Land-Rover, Solihull, England

CONFIGURATION: 4 × 4, front-engined station wagon

	doors	seats	unladen weight	max load
4-door	5	5	1760 kg (3880 lb)	750 kg (1653 lb)
2-door	3	5	1792 kg (3951 lb)	720 kg (1587 lb)

ENGINE: V-8, 3528 cc, water-cooled petrol with electronic ignition
i) High compression developing 125 bhp at 4000 rpm
| Torque | 258 Nm at 2500 rpm |
| Compression ratio | 9.35:1 |
ii) Low compression developing 130 bhp at 5000 rpm
| Torque | 251 Nm at 2500 rpm |
| Compression ratio | 8.13:1 |

TRANSMISSION: Manual or automatic. Permanent 4 × 4 with lockable central differential
Type of clutch	single dry plate
Number of gear ratios	5 forward, 1 reverse (manual)
Transfer box	2-speed

CHASSIS AND SUSPENSION: Box section ladder type chassis. Rubber-mounted steel body frame clad in aluminium panels. Long travel coil springs all round with hydraulic long stroke shock absorbers. Rear suspension incorporates self-levelling unit

Fuel tank	82 litres (18.04 gallons)
Brakes	discs all round with power assist, dual circuit at front, mechanical parking brake on transfer box rear shaft
Tyres	6.00 × 16 or 7.00 × 16
Electrical system	12V

DIMENSIONS:
Length	4.47 m (14 ft 8 in)
Width	1.78 m (5 ft 10 in)
Height	1.8 m (5 ft 11 in)
Wheelbase	2.54 m (8 ft 4 in)
Track	1.49 m (4 ft 11 in)
Turning radius	5.95 m (19 ft)
Ground clearance	0.19 m (7 in)
Angle of approach/departure	45°/35°

PERFORMANCE:
Max speed	155 km/h (96 mph)

Glamour chariot for the Middle East – the Glenfrome 'Facet'. Underneath it's a Range Rover

LOHR FL500 and FL501

One of a distinct breed of lightweight four-wheel drive utility vehicles developed for airborne operations, the original FL500 (also known as the Fardier) serves with the French Army, Argentina and has been evaluated by the British Army. It shows the economy of engineering typical of airborne lightweights being able to carry a maximum load of 500 kg (1102 lb) including the driver or tow a trailer or weapon weighing up to 500 kg (1102 lb), or 800 kg (1764 lb) for the FL501. Six FL500s can be packed into a tactical transport aircraft such as a C-130 or Transall ready for air dropping, or 12 if palletised as cargo. A single vehicle can be loaded into an SA 300 Puma helicopter.

The engine is mounted transversely amidships and it drives the front and rear axles via cardan-driven central transmission units. The reinforced axles are made of light alloy and sprung by rubber and helicoidal springs mounted horizontally on each side of the chassis in two suspension boxes. The chassis is of tubular steel with aluminium decking with a folding roll bar behind the driver's seat.

The vehicle can be readily adapted for casualty evacuation, as an ammunition carrier and as an anti-tank vehicle mounting the Milan ATGW with six reload rounds. The latest version is the FL501 fitted with a 36 hp engine as standard.

MANUFACTURER: Lohr, Hangenbieten, France

CONFIGURATION: 4 × 4, mid-engined, open, air-portable platform

	doors	seats	unladen weight	max load
FL 501	–	1	680 kg (1499 lb)	500 kg (1102 lb)

ENGINE: Citroën AK 2 flat twin 602 cc petrol developing 29 hp at 6750 rpm (FL 500), FL 501 has 36 hp engine

LuAZ-969M

Marketed as a civilian vehicle but developed from a military prototype for a light, air-transportable utility vehicle, the LuAZ-969M replaced the earlier 969 model in production at the Lutsk plant in the Ukraine in 1981. The original vehicle was developed at the Zaporozhe Motor Vehicle Plant from a pilot model, the ZAZ-969, which used mechanical components from the ZAZ-966 passenger car of 1965 vintage. The project was moved to the Lutsk plant and production began in 1972 under the LuAZ-969 designation. There was also a 4 × 2 model and a four-door forward control model designated LuAZ-971.

The current vehicle has an engine of slightly greater power, shared with the ZAZ-968 passenger car and the driver can select all-wheel drive or 4 × 2 in which case the rear instead of the front axle is disengaged. A 200 kg (441 lb) capacity winch and 100 m (328 ft) of cable can be fitted. be fitted.

The vehicle's chassis is also used as the basis for the LuAZ-967M low silhouette amphibious ambulance which has an open, boat-like hull with room for two stretchers plus folding seats for walking wounded.

Lohr 501 with Milan anti-tank missile platoon

MANUFACTURER:	Lutsk Motor Vehicle Plant, Ukraine, USSR			
CONFIGURATION:	4 × 4, front-engined, open body with canvas top, folding screen			
		doors seats	unladen weight	max load
	969M	2 2	970 kg (2138 lb)	400 kg (882 lb)
	969	2 2	820 kg (1808 lb)	380 kg (838 lb)
	967	— 1 + 2	930 kg (2050 lb)	420 kg (926 lb)

ENGINE:	MeMz-946 V-4, air-cooled, 1198 cc petrol, developing 40 hp at 4200 rpm

TRANSMISSION:	Manual, 4 × 4 or 4 × 2 selectable by disengaging rear axle	
	Number of gear ratios	4 forward, 1 reverse
	Transfer box	2-speed

CHASSIS AND SUSPENSION:	All steel unitary construction, torsion bar suspension	
	Fuel tank	32 litres (7.04 gallons)
	Brakes	hydraulic, mechanical parking
	Tyres	4 + 1 spare, 5.90 × 13
	Electrical system	12V

DIMENSIONS:	Length	3.37 m (11 ft 1 in)
	Width	1.64 m (5 ft 5 in)
	Height	1.77 m (5 ft 10 in)
	Wheelbase	1.8 m (5 ft 11 in)
	Track	1.32 m (4 ft 4 in)
	Turning radius	3 m (10 ft)
	Ground clearance	0.3 m (1 ft)
	Fording	0.45 m (1 ft 6 in)
	Gradient	58%

PERFORMANCE:	Max speed	85 km/h (53 mph)
	Power-to-weight ratio	23.8 kg/hp (52.47 lb/hp)
	Fuel consumption	10 litres/100 km (2.2 gallons/62 miles)

TRANSMISSION:	Manual	
	Number of gear ratios	4 forward, 1 reverse

CHASSIS AND SUSPENSION:	Welded tubular chassis, aluminium body and load platform. Trailing arm suspension front and rear with helical spring and hydraulic shock absorbers	
	Brakes	discs all round
	Steering	rack and pinion
	Tyres	165 × 15
	Electrical system	12V

DIMENSIONS:	Length	2.375 m (7 ft 9 in)
	Width	1.5 m (4 ft 11 in)
	Height	2 m (6 ft 7 in) (to rollbar)
	Wheelbase	1.735 m (5 ft 8 in)
	Track	1.26 m (4 ft 2 in)
	Ground clearance	0.26 m (10 in)
	Fording	0.4 m (1 ft 4 in)
	Gradient	60%
	Angle of approach/departure	90°/90°

PERFORMANCE:	Max road speed	80 km/h (50 mph)
	Operating range	200 km (124 miles)

MERCEDES-BENZ G-SERIES

The G-Wagen can get down to serious business

Mercedes-Benz bided its time in coming to the light four-wheel drive market, seeing the British Range Rover open up a prestige market and US and Japanese manufacturers also discovering the formula before they launched the G-wagen on the civil market in early 1979.

In fact the vehicle had already been designed around a military requirement and was the loser in the 1977 competition against the VW Iltis for a new generation light vehicle for the West German armed forces. However, built by Peugeot as the P4, the vehicle won the French Army's contract to replace its postwar generation Hotchkiss M201s.

A company called Gelandewagenfahrzeug Gesellschaft (GFG) was established to build the vehicle jointly by Mercedes-Benz and Steyr-Daimler-Puch, the Austrian company that built the Haflinger and Pinzgauer, with a production facility at Graz in Austria. The Austrian end bought out Mercedes in 1981 but continues to build the vehicle under contract for civil and military customers with MB doing the marketing in all countries other than Austria, Switzerland, Yugoslavia and the Eastern bloc where it is sold under the Steyr-Daimler-Puch badge.

The mechanical components are made by Mercedes-Benz and, with the exception of the transfer case, come from passenger car and light truck production. The chassis and bodywork are made at Graz where final assembly takes place.

The design layout is conventional and engineered to a high standard with a choice of four engines in two wheel-bases with other options adding up to a range of 40 models. A box section chassis with tubular cross members provides an exceptionally tough framework with suspension engineered to a high standard to soak up the knocks. Rigid live axles front and rear are sprung by extra long coil springs allowing 260 mm (10 inches) of articulation with progressive hollow rubber assistor springs at the rear.

The long travel springs, the low centre of gravity and the minimum overhang, front and rear, are designed to give the optimum off-road handling and ensure the vehicle will slide rather than topple in a side-tilt. The doors are watertight and floor and engine are protected against water penetration to give a fording depth of 60 cm (2 ft). Optional equipment includes differential locks, front winch, front towing hook, trailer coupling, special heat insulation and ventilation, extra wide tyres, spare tyre cover, headlight washer, heat insulating glass, additional heater for extremely low temperature operations, power assisted steering, halogen foglamps, spotlight and spare wheel on swivelling bracket.

So far the military versions of the G-wagen have entered service with Argentina, Norway and France (as the Peugeot P4). Some captured vehicles have been used by the British garrison in the Falkland Islands.

MANUFACTURER: Daimler Benz AG Stuttgart, Unterturkheim, West Germany, production by GFG, Graz, Austria

CONFIGURATION: 4 ×4, front-engined, open body with canvas top, station wagon, van

	doors	seats	unladen weight	max load
Station wagon	3	5–7	1935 kg (4266 lb)	850 kg (1874 lb)
Station wagon (lwb)	5	9	2055 kg (4530 lb)	750 kg (1653 lb)
Van	3	2	1885 kg (4156 lb)	540 kg (1190 lb)
Van (lwb)	3	2	1965 kg (4332 lb)	760 kg (1675 lb)
Pick-up	2	5	1885 kg (4156 lb)	915 kg (2017 lb)

CHASSIS AND SUSPENSION: Box section chassis to which all steel body is bolted. Rigid axles front and rear with long travel coil springs. Front and rear axles located by 1 transverse Panhard rod and 2 longitudinal control rods

Fuel tank	70 litres (15.4 gallons) (including 1 litre (2.42 gallons) reserve)
Brakes	discs at front, power-assisted drum at rear with automatic load-sensitive power control
Steering	toothed sector recirculating ball, power assist optional
Tyres	7.00 ×16
Electrical system	24V

DIMENSIONS:

Pick-up
Length	3.955 m (13 ft)
Width	1.7 m (5 ft 7 in)
Height	1.945 m (6 ft 5 in)
Wheelbase	2.4 m (7 ft 10 in)
Track	1.425 m (4 ft 8 in)
Turning radius	5.7 m (19 ft)
Ground clearance	0.21 m (8 in)
Fording	0.6 m (2 ft)
Gradient	80%
Angle of approach/departure	36°/31°

Station wagon
Length	4.11 m (13 ft 6 in)
Width	1.7 m (5 ft 7 in)
Height	1.925 m (6 ft 4 in)
Wheelbase	2.4 m (7 ft 10 in)

Station wagon (Lwb)
Length	4.56 m (14 ft 11 in)
Width	1.7 m (5 ft 7 in)
Height	1.92 m (6 ft 4 in)
Wheelbase	2.85 m (9 ft 4 in)

– yet retains all the glamour of a Mercedes

ENGINE: There are four engine options for pick-up, station wagon and van in the two wheelbases – the 240 GD (2.4-litre diesel). 300 GD (3-litre diesel), 230 G (2.3-litre petrol) and 280 GE (2.8-litre petrol with fuel injection). Fuel injection has been offered on the 230 GE from 1982 onwards

240 GD:
Daimler Benz OM616, 4-cylinder, 2399 cc, water-cooled, in-line diesel producing 72 hp at 4400 rpm
Torque	137 Nm at 2400 rpm
Compression ratio	21:1

TRANSMISSION: Manual or automatic. Selectable 4 ×2 or 4 ×4, optional differential lock
Type of clutch	single dry plate
Number of gear ratios	5 forward, 1 reverse

1) 3.822:1   2) 2.199:1   3) 1.398:1   4) 1:1
5) 0.813:1   Rev. 4.348:1   Final drive 5.33:1
Transfer box	2-speed giving reduction of 2.14:1

PERFORMANCE:
Max speed	120 km/h (75 mph)
Power-to-weight ratio	25.1 kg/hp (55.34 lb/hp)
Fuel consumption	11.8–14.1 litres/100 km (2.6–3.1 gallons/62 miles)

ENGINE: 300 GD
Mercedes Benz OM617, 5-cylinder, 2998 cc, water-cooled, in-line diesel producing 88 hp at 4400 rpm
Torque	172 Nm at 2400 rpm
Compression ratio	21:1

TRANSMISSION: As 240 GD

PERFORMANCE:
Max speed	130 km/h (81 mph)
Power-to-weight ratio	21.4 kg/hp (47.18 lb/hp)
Fuel consumption	11.7–14.6 litres/100 km (2.57–3.21 gallons/62 miles)

ENGINE: 230 G
Daimler Benz M115, 4-cylinder, 2308 cc, in-line, water-cooled developing 90 hp at 5000 rpm
Torque	172 Nm at 2500 rpm
Compression ratio	9:1

(optional 9:1 compression engine producing 102 hp at 5250 rpm)

TRANSMISSION: As 240 GD

PERFORMANCE:
Max speed	137 km/h (85 mph) (128 km/h (79 mph) low compression engine)
Power-to-weight ratio	17.8 kg/hp (39.24 lb/hp)
Fuel consumption	12.5–19.2 litres/100 km (2.75–4.22 gallons/62 miles) (12.2–18.8 litres/100 km (2.68–4.13 gallons/62 miles))

ENGINE: 230 GE
Daimler Benz M115 E23, 4-cylinder, 2299 cc, water-cooled, in-line with fuel injection developing 125 hp at 5000 rpm
Torque	192 Nm at 4000 rpm
Compression ratio	9:1

TRANSMISSION: As 240 GD, final drive 4.9:1

PERFORMANCE:
Max speed	143 km/h (89 mph)
Power-to-weight ratio	14.6 kg/hp (32.19 lb/hp)

ENGINE: 280 GE
Daimler Benz M110E, 4-cylinder, 2746 cc, water-cooled, in-line with fuel injection developing 156 hp at 5250 rpm
Torque	226 Nm at 4250 rpm
Compression ratio	8:1

PERFORMANCE:
Max speed	155 km/h (96 mph)
Power-to-weight ratio	16.6 kg/hp (36.6 lb/hp)
Fuel consumption	13.1–21.5 litres/100 km (2.88–4.73 gallons/62 miles)

MITSUBISHI JEEPS

During the Pacific war Japanese armed forces used the little Kurogane Type 95 Scout Car plus larger four-wheel drive versions of passenger touring cars. Captured US Jeeps were prized forms of transport and Toyota put a copy of a captured US Bantam into production right at the war's end and built five pilot models, eventually to emerge as the Toyota Model BJ, sire of the Land Cruiser line.

In 1953 the reconstructed Mitsubishi concern obtained a licence from the Willys company to produce Jeeps in Japan for civil and military use. The Japanese Self Defence Forces were constituted in 1954 and generated a requirement for light military vehicles. The first such model was the CJ-3B-J3, followed by many other models in left and right hand drive, long or short wheelbases, and with petrol or diesel engines. The CJ-3B differed from the CJ-3B-J4 for example in having 24- instead of 12-volt electrics while other models mounted recoilless rifles or have been adapted as field ambulances or anti-tank missile launchers.

The current Mitsubishi Jeep range covers the J56 powered by a four-cylinder petrol engine and the J24 powered by a four-cylinder diesel, both with a wheelbase of 2.225 m (7 ft 4 in), and the J38 and J46 powered by petrol engines on a 2.64-m (8 ft 8 in) wheelbase and the J36 and J55 powered by diesel engines on the longer wheelbase.

Civil vehicles are marketed with canvas top and open body or station wagon hard top with five doors on three wheelbases.

MITSUBISHI PAJERO, COLT SHOGUN

Launched in 1981, the Shogun (the name under which the vehicle is marketed in Great Britain) is midway between the small Japanese 4 × 4, the Suzukis and Daihatsus, and the big Range Rover/Land Cruiser estates. Success in the 1983 Paris–Dakar rally showed the toughness of the design while the level of saloon-car luxury is high. A 2.3-litre turbo-diesel was introduced in 1983 and a five-door station wagon on a long wheelbase in 1983.

MANUFACTURER:	Mitsubishi Motor Corporation, Tokyo, Japan			
CONFIGURATION:	4 × 4, front-engined, open body with canvas top, station wagon on two wheelbases			
		doors	seats	unladen weight	max load
	Open body (swb)	2	5	1380 kg (3042 lb)	735 kg (1620 lb)
	Station wagon	3	5	1415 kg (3119 lb)	710 kg (1565 lb)
	Station wagon (lwb)	5	7	1450 kg (3197 lb)	750 kg (1653 lb)

ENGINE:	i) 4-cylinder, 1997 cc, water-cooled petrol, developing 110 hp at 5500 rpm
	Torque 164 Nm at 3500 rpm
	Compression ratio 8.5:1
	ii) 4-cylinder, 1997 cc, water-cooled petrol with turbo-charging developing 145 hp at 5500 rpm
	Torque 164 Nm at 3500 rpm
	Compression ratio 8.5:1
	iii) 4-cylinder, 2555 cc, water-cooled petrol developing 120 hp at 5000 rpm
	Torque 208 Nm at 3000 rpm
	Compression ratio 8.2:1
	iv) 4-cylinder, 2346 cc, water-cooled diesel developing 75 hp at 4200 rpm
	Torque 175 Nm at 2500 rpm
	Compression ratio 21:1
	v) 4-cylinder, 2346 cc, water-cooled diesel with turbo-charging developing 95 hp at 4200 rpm
	Torque 181 Nm at 2500 rpm
	Compression ratio 21:1

TRANSMISSION:	Manual, selectable 4 × 4 or 4 × 2, automatic front freewheeling hubs	
	Type of clutch	single dry plate
	Number of gear ratios	5 forward, 1 reverse
	1) 3.74:1 2) 2.136:1 3) 1.36:1 4) 1:1	
	5) 0.586:1 Rev. 3.578:1 Final drive 4.875:1	
	(2-litre turbo 4.625:1)	
	Transfer box	2-speed 1:1/1.944:1

CHASSIS AND SUSPENSION:	Box section ladder type with steel body. Independent front suspension by coil springs. Rear leaf springs, telescopic shock absorbers all round	
	Fuel tank	60 litres (13.19 gallons)
	Brakes	discs front, drums rear with servo
	Steering	recirculating ball with power assist
	Tyres	215 SR × 15
	Electrical system	12V

DIMENSIONS:	Swb	
	Length	3.87 m (12 ft 8 in)
	Width	1.68 m (5 ft 6 in)
	Height	1.88 m (6 ft 2 in)
	Wheelbase	2.35 m (7 ft 8 in)
	Track	1.4 m/1.375 m (rear) (4 ft 7 in/4 ft 6 in (rear)
	Turning radius	5.9 m (19 ft)
	Ground clearance	0.235 m (9 in)
	Lwb	
	Length	4.535 m (14 ft 10 in)
	Width	1.68 m (5 ft 6 in)
	Height	1.98 m (6 ft 6 in)
	Wheelbase	2.695 m (8 ft 10 in)
	Track	1.4 m/1.375 m (rear) (4 ft 7 in/4 ft 6 in)
	Turning radius	5.9 m (19 ft)
	Ground clearance	0.235 m (9 in)

PERFORMANCE:	2.6-litre petrol	
	Max speed	140 km/h (87 mph)
	Power-to-weight ratio	13.5 kg/hp (29.76 lb/hp)
	Fuel consumption	12–18 litres/100 km (2.63–3.95 gallons/62 miles)

PERFORMANCE:	2.3-litre turbo diesel	
	Max speed	130 km/h (81 mph)
	Fuel consumption	10–15 litres/100 km (2.19–3.29 gallons/62 miles)

The petrol driven Shogun, sold as the 'Pajero' in certain markets

Mitsubishi Colt Shogun diesel turbo

The Colt Shogun is one of the most handsome of '80s four wheel drives

NISSAN PATROL/SAFARI

Nissan Patrol of mid-'60s vintage

Nissan have been making four-wheel drive vehicles under the 'Patrol' label since the early 1950s. The first were clearly modelled on the wartime Willys MB but were extensively improved and developed through the 1960s with a full width boxy bodywork, hard top station wagon and long wheelbase station wagon models. The vehicle was licence manufactured in India as the Jonga.

The series was relaunched in 1980 with new bodywork and is available as a hard top on long wheelbase station wagon. In 1983 an optional turbocharged 3.25-litre diesel was introduced. The vehicle is marketed internationally as the Datsun Patrol or Nissan Safari and is licence-built in Spain.

MANUFACTURER:	Nissan Motor Company, Tokyo, Japan		

CONFIGURATION:	4 × 4, front-engined station wagon on two wheelbases		
	doors	**seats**	**unladen weight**
swb	3	5	1670 kg (3681 lb)
lwb	5	5	1965 kg (4332 lb)

ENGINE:	
i) 6-cylinder, 2753 cc, water-cooled petrol developing 120 bhp at 4800 rpm	
Torque	213 Nm at 3600 rpm
Torque	213 Nm at 3600 rpm
Compression ratio	6.8:1
ii) 6-cylinder, 3246 cc, water-cooled diesel developing 95 bhp at 3600 rpm	
Torque	216 Nm at 1800 rpm
Compression ratio	20.8:1
iii) 6-cylinder, 3246 cc, water-cooled diesel with turbo-charging developing 120 hp at 4000 rpm	
Torque	265 Nm at 2000 rpm

TRANSMISSION:	Manual, selectable 4 × 2 or 4 × 4, 4-speed for 4 speed box	
Type of clutch	single dry plate
Number of gear ratios	i) 4 forward, 1 reverse
1) 4.222:1 2) 2.37:1 3) 1.44:1 4) 1:1 Rev. 4.622:1	
	ii) 5 forward, 1 reverse
1) 3.895:1 2) 2.37:1 3) 1.44:1 4) 1:1 5) 0.825:1 Rev. 4.267:1	
Final drive (5-speed)	4.375:1
Transfer box	2-speed

CHASSIS AND SUSPENSION:	Ladder type, with steel and glass fibre body. Semi-elliptical leaf springs all round with hydraulic shock absorbers, rigid axles	
Fuel tank	85 litres (18.69 gallons)
Brakes	discs front, drums rear, with power assist
Steering	recirculating ball with power assist
Tyres	6.50 × 16
Electrical system	12V

DIMENSIONS:	Length	4.07 m (13 ft 4 in)
	Width	1.69 m (5 ft 6 in)
	Height	1.84 m (6 ft)
	Wheelbase	2.35 m (7 ft 8 in) (hard top) 2.97 m (9 ft 9 in) (station wagon)
	Track	1.4 m/1.41 m (rear) (4 ft 7 in/4 ft 7 in)
	Turning radius	5.8 m (19 ft)
	Ground clearance	0.23 m (9 in)

PERFORMANCE:	Max speed (petrol)	150 km/h (93 mph)
	Power-to-weight ratio	11.2 kg/hp (24.69 lb/hp)
	Fuel consumption	11.1–17 litres/100 km
	(Hard top)	(2.44–3.73 gallons/62 miles)
	(Station wagon)	12.7–18.9 litres/100 km (2.79–4.15 gallons/62 miles)
	Max speed (diesel)	130 km/h (81 mph)
	Power-to-weight ratio	15.3 kg/hp (33.73 lb/hp)
	Fuel consumption	12–20 litres/100 km (2.63–4.39 gallons/62 miles)

By 1984 the Patrol had evolved into a crisply styled, sophisticated vehicle

The Patrol is also available as a four-door, long wheelbase high roofline model

Peugeot 504 pickup modified to 4 × 4 by the French engineering firm of Dangel

PEUGEOT 504 (DANGEL)

Peugeot 504 Dangel estate

The Dangel company of Sentheim, in eastern France, manufactures four-wheel drive conversions of the Citroën Visa and of the rugged Peugeot 504 in pick-up, estate and ambulance variants for the French Navy and Marines, and for sale in African markets which are particularly important for Peugeot.

The front and rear axles have Peugeot limited slip differentials with the Dangel transfer case mounted in the transmission tunnel but independent of the main propshaft due to a short universal jointed shaft turning in the reaction tube. The Dangel transfer case affords four road and four additional cross-country gears and transfer can be made while the vehicle is on the move.

Other modifications include additional underbody protection, stiffening chassis longerons, plus a front-mounted winch; otherwise the vehicles are standard. The pick-up has a fixed head enclosed cab with canvas cover for the rear load area. The ambulance has a conformal rear cab which fits over the pick-up area accommodating three stretcher and two seated patients.

ENGINE:	i) Peugeot XNI, water-cooled, 1971 cc petrol developing 96 hp at 5200 rpm ii) Peugeot XD2 water-cooled, 2304 cc diesel developing 70 hp at 4500 rpm
TRANSMISSION:	Manual, permanent 4-wheel drive
	Type of clutch — single dry plate
	Number of gear ratios — 4 forward, 1 reverse
	Transfer box — Dangel PO3 2-speed
CHASSIS AND SUSPENSION:	Ladder frame chassis directly bolted to unitary construction body. Reinforced coil springs all round (break), semi-elliptical leaf springs rear (pick-up)
	Fuel tank — 60 litres (13.2 gallons)
	Brakes — discs front, drums rear, double circuit
	Steering — rack and pinion
	Tyres — 5.5 × 16
	Electrical system — 12V
DIMENSIONS:	Station wagon
	Length — 4.8 m (15 ft 9 in)
	Width — 1.73 m (5 ft 8 in)
	Height — 1.74 m (5 ft 8 in)
	Wheelbase — 2.91 m (9 ft 7 in)
	Track — 1.49/1.36 m (rear) (4 ft 11 in/4 ft 5 in)
	Turning radius — 5.7 m (19 ft)
	Ground clearance — 0.215 m (8 in)
	Angle of approach/departure — 45°/30°
	Pick-up
	Length — 4.758 m (15 ft 7 in)
	Width — 1.77 m (5 ft 10 in)
	Wheelbase — 3.017 m (9 ft 11 in)
PERFORMANCE:	Max speed — 146 km/h (petrol) (91 mph)
	Power-to-weight ratio — 15.8 kg/hp (34.83 lb/hp)
	Fuel consumption — 9.6–13.1 litres/100 km (2.11–2.88 gallons/62 miles)

MANFACTURER:	Automobiles Peugeot/Automobiler Dangel, Sentheim, France				
CONFIGURATION:		doors	seats	unladen weight	max load
	Break	5	5	1525 kg (3362 lb)	1970 kg (4343 lb)
	Break Familial	5	6	1525 kg (3362 lb)	1970 kg (4343 lb)
	Pick-up	2	3	1405 kg (3097 lb)	1110 kg (2447 lb)

PEUGEOT P4

Peugeot P4 of the French Army with HOT anti-tank missile

With the collapse of the 'Euro-Jeep' project, France was still left with a need to replace the Hotchkiss M201 wartime Jeep derivative. Three French manufacturers went after the prize, in fact using nationally-built versions of foreign vehicles: the Renault TRM 500 (the Italian Fiat 1107 AD), the Citroën C44 based on the VW Iltis and the Peugeot P4 based on the Mercedes-Benz G-wagen which had competed unsuccessfully with the Volkswagen for a similar West German Army requirement.

In the event it was the Peugeot submission which was announced the winner in 1981 with a French Army order for 15,000 vehicles before 1987.

The vehicle is conventional with a separate chassis and steel body, front-mounted engine, rear cargo area, folding canvas top and windscreen. The front seats are adjustable with the refinement of inertia reel seat belts, hinging forward to give access to the rear and with tool boxes beneath each of them. The bench seats in the rear can be folded away to give an unrestricted cargo area.

The P4 comes in short and long wheelbase versions either open or hard top and in military service has been tested with a variety of automatic weapons and Milan ATGWs. Optional equipment includes either petrol or diesel engines, power steering, a front locking differential, power take-off at front and rear, electric winch and 15-litre (3.3 gallons) fuel can.

ENGINE:	Peugeot 4-cylinder, 1971 cc, petrol developing 79 hp at 4750 rpm or Peugeot 4-cylinder, 2498 cc, diesel developing 70 bhp at 4500 rpm	
TRANSMISSION:	Manual	
	Type of clutch	single dry plate
	Number of gear ratios	4 forward, 1 reverse
	Transfer box	2-speed
CHASSIS AND SUSPENSION:	Box section chassis to which steel body is bolted. Rigid axles front and rear with long travel coil springs and hydraulic double-acting shock absorbers	
	Fuel tank	75 litres (16.5 gallons)
	Brakes	discs front, drums rear, hydraulic dual circuit
	Steering	rack and pinion
	Tyres	7.00 × 16
	Electrical system	24V
DIMENSIONS:	Swb	
	Length	4.2 m (13 ft 9 in)
	Width	1.6 m (5 ft 7 in)
	Height	1.9 m (6 ft 3 in)
	Wheelbase	2.4 m (7 ft 10 in)
	Track	1.4 m (4 ft 7 in)
	Turning radius	5.5 m (18 ft)
	Ground clearance	0.24 m (9 in)
	Fording	0.5 m (1 ft 8 in)
	Gradient	73.5% (petrol)
	Angle of approach/departure	42°/37°
	Lwb	
	Length	4.65 m (15 ft 3 in)
	Width	1.7 m (5 ft 7 in)
	Height	1.9 m (6 ft 3 in)
	Wheelbase	2.85 m (9 ft 4 in)
	Track	1.4 m (4 ft 7 in)
	Turning radius	6.45 m (21 ft)
	Ground clearance	0.24 m (9 in)
	Fording	0.5 m (1 ft 8 in)
	Gradient	55% (diesel)
	Angle of approach/departure	42°/37°
PERFORMANCE:	Max speed (petrol)	118 km/h (73 mph)
	(diesel)	108 km/h (67 mph)
	Fuel consumption	23.3 litres/100 km (petrol) (5.12 gallons/62 miles), 18 litres/100 km (diesel) (3.96 gallons/62 miles)

MANUFACTURER: Automobiles Peugeot, Paris, France

CONFIGURATION: 4 × 4, front-engined open body with canvas or hard top

	doors	seats	unladen weight	max load
swb	2	2 + 6	1815 kg (4001 lb)	750 kg (1653 lb)
lwb	2	2 + 8	1985 kg (4376 lb)	750 kg (1653 lb)

PORTARO 260

Manufactured in Portugal since 1975, based originally on the Romanian ARO, the Portaro has been developed into a sophisticated range of vehicles with independent front suspension and a turbo diesel engine offered in the top of the range Celta. The 260D has an open body, the 260DP is a hard top pick-up, the 260DCM Furgo is a van model, the 260DCM utility nine-seater a station wagon, the 320 a long wheelbase dropside pick-up, and the top of the range 260 Celta, 210PT Celta turbo and 260 Celta turbo diesel pick-up/hard top station wagons. Engines are Daihatsu diesels or Volvo B23A petrol.

MANUFACTURER:	Sociadad Electro-Mecanicada Automoveis, Lisbon, Portugal

CONFIGURATION: 4 × 4, front-engined, pick-up, with hard top, station wagon

	doors	seats	unladen weight	max load
Station wagon	3	9	1650 kg (3638 lb)	880 kg (1940 lb)

ENGINE:	i) Daihatsu, 2530 cc, water-cooled diesel developing 72 hp at 6000 rpm
	Torque 172 Nm at 2200 rpm
	Compression ratio 21:1

TRANSMISSION: Manual, selectable 4 × 2 or 4 × 4
Type of clutch   single dry plate
Number of gear ratios   4 forward, 1 reverse
1) 3.717:1   2) 2.177:1   3) 1.513:1   4) 1:1
Rev. 4.34:1   Final drive 3.7:1
Transfer box   2-speed   1.30:1/2.407:1

CHASSIS AND SUSPENSION: Box section ladder frame. Independent front suspension by coil springs with telescopic shock absorbers, rigid rear axle, semi-elliptical leaf springs with telescopic shock absorbers
Fuel tank   95 litres (20.89 gallons)
Brakes   drums all round
Steering   recirculating ball, power assist optional
Tyres   6.50 × 16
Electrical system   12V

DIMENSIONS:
Length   4 m (13 ft 1 in)
Width   1.78 m (5 ft 10 in)
Height   1.98 m (6 ft 6 in)
Wheelbase   2.35 m (7 ft 8 in)
Track   1.44 m (4 ft 9 in)
Turning radius   6 m (20 ft)
Ground clearance   0.22 m (9 in)
Fording   0.6 m (2 ft)
Gradient   60%

PERFORMANCE:
Max speed   112 km/h (70 mph)
Power-to-weight ratio   22.9 kg/hp (50.48 lb/hp)
Fuel consumption   11 litres/100 km (2.41 gallons/62 miles)

Portaro 260 Celta

QT JEG TL

Lightweight utility four-wheel drive making extensive use of VW do Brasil components including floor pan, suspension, transmission and engine which is aircooled and rear-mounted in the classic Beetle mould. The Jeg is offered as an open-body soft top or three-door hard top.

MANUFACTURER:	QT Engenharia e Eqipamentos, São Paulo, Brazil

CONFIGURATION: 4 × 4, rear-engined, open body with canvas top, station wagon

	doors	seats	unladen weight	max load
Station wagon	3	5	1800 kg (3968 lb)	590 kg (1300 lb)

ENGINE: Volkswagen 4-cylinder, 1584 cc, air-cooled petrol, developing 55 hp at 4200 rpm
Torque 106 Nm at 3000 rpm
Compression ratio 7.2:1
(Optional ethyl alcohol engine, optional fuel injection)

TRANSMISSION:	Manual	
	Type of clutch	single dry plate
	Number of gear ratios	4 forward, 1 reverse
	1) 3.8:1 2) 2.06:1 3) 1.32:1 4) 0.88:1	
	Rev. 3.88:1 Final drive 5.143:1	

CHASSIS AND SUSPENSION: Box section ladder frame. Independent front suspension via transverse torsion bars with telescopic shock absorbers. Independent rear suspension via longitudinal torsion bars

	Fuel tank	55 litres (12.09 gallons)
	Brakes	drums all round
	Steering	worm and roller
	Tyres	7.35 × 15
	Electrical system	12V

DIMENSIONS:	Length	3.3 m (10 ft 10 in)
	Width	1.65 m (5 ft 5 in)
	Height	1.7 m (5 ft 7 in)
	Wheelbase	2 m (6 ft 7 in)
	Track	1.46 m/1.5 m (rear) (4 ft 9 in/4 ft 11 in)
	Turning radius	6 m (20 ft)
	Ground clearance	0.25 m (10 in)

PERFORMANCE:	Max speed	104 km/h (65 mph)
	Power-to-weight ratio	18.1 kg/hp (39.9 lb/hp)
	Fuel consumption	10.8 litres/100 km (2.37 gallons/62 miles)

RENAULT 18 BREAK

Renault have been in the business of making four-wheel drive versions of their standard passenger cars since the early 1950s; offering 'Tous Terrains' variants largely for colonial markets. The specialist engineering firm of Sinpar based at Colombes near Paris began making conversions of the ubiquitous Renault R4 in 1964 plus the Rodeo recreational vehicle on the R4 floor pan and progressed later to the R6 offering military derivatives of the larger vehicle. The tradition continues in the Renault R18 station wagon launched in 1982 pointed firmly at the dual purpose 'snowbelt' market if not the old days of workhorses for the colonies.

MANUFACTURER:	Renault, Billancourt, France

CONFIGURATION: 4 × 4, front-engined, station wagon

	doors	seats	unladen weight	max load
18 Break	5	5	1070 kg (2359 lb)	420 kg (926 lb)

ENGINE: i) 4-cylinder, 1647 cc, water-cooled petrol developing 74 hp at 5000 rpm
Torque 130 Nm at 3000 rpm
Compression ratio 9.3:1
ii) 4-cylinder, 2068 cc, water-cooled diesel developing 66 hp at 4500 rpm
Torque 127 Nm at 2250 rpm
Compression ratio 21.5:1

TRANSMISSION:	Manual, selectable 4 × 4 or 4 × 2	
	Type of clutch	single dry plate
	Number of gear ratios	5 forward, 1 reverse
	1) 4.091:1 2) 2.176:1 3) 1.409:1 4) 0.97:1	
	5) 0.78:1 Rev. 3.545:1 Final drive 3.778:1	

CHASSIS AND SUSPENSION:	Fuel tank	57 litres (12.53 gallons)
	Brakes	discs front, drums rear, with servo
	Steering	rack and pinion, power assist optional
	Tyres	165SR 13
	Electrical system	12V

DIMENSIONS:	Length	4.485 m (14 ft 8 in)
	Width	1.68 m (5 ft 6 in)
	Height	1.4 m (4 ft 7 in)
	Wheelbase	2.43 m (8 ft)
	Track	1.415 m/1.355 m (rear) (4 ft 8 in/4 ft 6 in)
	Turning radius	5.45 m (18 ft)
	Ground clearance	0.165 m (6 in)

PERFORMANCE:	75 hp petrol	
	Max speed	150 km/h (93 mph)
	Power-to-weight ratio	14.5 kg/hp (31.96 lb/hp)
	Fuel consumption	5.7–9 litres/100 km (1.25–1.97 gallons/62 miles)
	66 hp diesel	
	Max speed	148 km/h (92 mph)
	Power-to-weight ratio	18 kg/hp (39.68 lb/hp)
	Fuel consumption	5.4–8.5 litres/100 km (1.18–1.86 gallons/62 miles)

SIMI COURNIL

Samo military trucks drawn up outside the factory

The Tracteur Cournil concern was founded by a French engineer, Bernard Cournil, in the late 1950s building an agricultural utility vehicle powered by various proprietary engines and with surplus Jeep gearboxes and running gear. Hotchkiss and Renault petrol engines were offered and Hotchkiss and Indenor diesels and the Cournil 4 × 4 light truck was sold to French farmers in small numbers and some reached markets in Africa. The Marseilles fire brigade adapted them as fire tenders.

The design was taken over by the Gevelot concern which developed the vehicle mechanically and began to market it more aggressively and in 1977 it offered a military line called SAMO, essentially the Cournil in military guise.

Gevelot in turn was taken over by SIMI which was transformed again into Autoland in 1984. The Cournil meanwhile is still offered in short and long wheelbases in a variety of body styles including open truck, pick-up and hard top. In 1984 a new model with a redesigned front end was launched on the civil market, called the Tropic.

ENGINE:	i) Peugeot XD20 4-cylinder, 2340 cc, water-cooled diesel developing 67.4 hp at 4000 rpm (Models SCD 15, SCD 25)
	ii) Renault 829 4-cylinder, 1995 cc, water-cooled petrol developing 83 hp at 5000 rpm (Models SCE 15, SCE 25, SCE 25L)
	iii) Saviem 720 4-cylinder 3595 cc, water-cooled diesel developing 85 hp at 3000 rpm (Model SCD 28L)

TRANSMISSION:	Manual, selectable 4 × 4 or 4 × 2	
	Type of clutch	single dry plate
	Number of gear ratios	4 forward, 1 reverse
	Transfer box	2-speed

CHASSIS AND SUSPENSION:	Ladder type box section chassis, semi-elliptical leaf springs all round with hydraulic shock absorbers all round	
	Fuel tank	60 litres (13.2 gallons)
	Brakes	drum brakes all round, dual circuit
	Steering	worm and roller
	Tyres	6.50 × 16
	Electrical system	12V

DIMENSIONS:	Length	3.6 m (11 ft 10 in) (swb)
		4.23 m (13 ft 10 in) (lwb)
	Width	1.592 m (5 ft 3 in)
	Height	1.9 m (6 ft 3 in)
	Wheelbase	2.04 m (6 ft 8 in) (swb),
		2.54 m (8 ft 4 in) (lwb)
	Track	1.35 m/1.275 m (rear)
		(4 ft 5 in/4 ft 2 in)
	Turning radius	5.5 m (18 ft)
	Ground clearance	0.216 m (8 in)
	Fording	0.6 m (2 ft)
	Gradient	60%
	Angle of approach/departure	42°/35° (swb)

| PERFORMANCE: | Max speed | 107.56 km/h (67 mph) |

MANUFACTURER: SIMI, GI-Germain-Laval, France

CONFIGURATION: 4 × 4, front-engined, open truck body, soft canvas top or hard top

	doors	seats	unladen weight	max load
SCD 15	2	–	1490 kg	730 kg
			(3285 lb)	(1609 lb)
SCE 25	2	–	1622 kg	770 kg
			(3576 lb)	(1698 lb)
SCO 28L	2	–	1800 kg	1500 kg
			(3968 lb)	(3307 lb)

Renault 18 Break 4 × 4

SAMO

The Cournil is a tough, conventionally engineered light truck, a Samo restyled for the civil market in 1983

Very much a light truck as much as a field car, the SAMO was developed in the mid-seventies by SAMO and Gevarm from the Cournil design as a light tactical military vehicle available with various powerplants and highly adaptable to a wide range of roles. So far the vehicle has found export customers in several African armies and is now manufactured by the Société Internationale de Materiels Industriels (SIMI).

There are two basic versions in long and short wheelbase, both with a conventional ladder type box section chassis to which the sheet steel body is directly welded. Saviem, Renault and Peugeot engines are offered.

The layout is conventional with a front engine and rear cargo area with bench seats down each side and tailgate. The basic model has forward folding windscreen and removable canvas top and doors while a hard top is available for both wheelbase lengths.

Variants include ambulance and command and communications vehicle while the standard model can mount various automatic weapons. The Lwb version can mount 200 mm cannon, recoilless rifles or anti-tank guided weapons.

Optional equipment for both civil and military applications include 24-volt electrics, wider tread tyres, a 3500 kg (7716 lb) winch, power take-off, oil cooler, power steering, brakes and clutch, overdrive, heater, rhd, heavy duty axles, extra fuel tanks, sump, gearbox and fuel tank guards, desert and tropical filters and ventilation, drinking water tank and deep wading exhaust.

SBARRO WIND HOUND and WIND HAWK

The office of the pricey Sbarro Windhound resembles the cockpit of a light aircraft

The Swiss firm of Sbarro specialises in building ultra-exotic and expensive 'replicars' based on classics such as the Mercedes 540K roadster and Ford GT40 Le Mans. It entered the luxury four-wheel drive field with an eye to Middle East markets, launching the Windhound at the 1978 Paris Motor Show. The vehicle uses Mercedes running gear, some Fiat chassis components and the engine is at the choice of the customer although the manufacturers offer BMW, Ford, Mercedes and Jeep Cherokee V-8 units. The ground clearance can be hydraulically adjusted from within the vehicle and two- and four-door bodies are offered.

The six-wheel Wind Hawk was developed as a hunting vehicle for a Middle Eastern ruler. A special hunting platform emerges through the roof by hydraulic action.

ENGINE:	BMW, Ford, Mercedes, Jeep Cherokee or others developing 150–270 hp		
TRANSMISSION:	Automatic or 4–5 speed manual		
	Type of clutch	single dry plate	
	Number of gear ratios	4–5 forward, 1 reverse	
	Transfer box	2-speed	
CHASSIS AND SUSPENSION:	Unitary body with subframes (Wind Hawk has ladder frame steel tube chassis), independent suspension all round by transverse torsion bars		
	Fuel tank	80 litres (17.6 gallons) (Wind Hound), 350 litres (76.99 gallons) (Wind Hawk)	
	Brakes	drums all round, discs at front optional	
	Steering	power assisted	
	Tyres	12 × 15	
	Electrical system	12V	
DIMENSIONS:	(Wind Hound)		
	Length		
	Width	1.81 m (5 ft 11 in)	
	Height	1.7 m (5 ft 7 in)	
	Wheelbase	2.7 m (8 ft 10 in)	
	Track	1.49 m/1.51 m (rear) (4 ft 11 in/4 ft 11 in)	
	Ground clearance	0.27 m–0.49 m (11 in–1 ft 7 in)	
PERFORMANCE:	Max speed	180–200 km/h (112–124 mph) depending on engine	

MANUFACTURER: ACA Sbarro, Tuilleries de Grandson, Switzerland

CONFIGURATION: 4 × 4, station wagon, 6 × 6 station wagon

	doors	seats	unladen weight
Wind Hound	3	5	2000 kg (4409 lb)
Wind Hound	5	5	2000 kg (4409 lb)
Wind Hawk	5	8	2400 kg (5291 lb)

Sbarro Windhound – exclusive four wheel drive at a price

STEYR-DAIMLER-700AP HAFLINGER

One of the most famous of post-war four-wheel drive vehicles, the Austrian Haflinger, named after a tough breed of Austrian mountain pony, was in production from 1959–74 and is still in widespread military service with many examples in civil hands and a loyal enthusiast following.

The vehicle was designed by Erich Ledwinka, Chief Designer at Steyr-Daimler-Puch and son of Hans Ledwinka, the legendary Czech engineer. Hans Ledwinka had worked for Steyr during and after the First World War and had produced the revolutionary Tatra cars and trucks of the 1920s and 1930s with such features as tubular backbone chassis, independent suspension, air-cooled engines and close attention to aerodynamics.

The Haflinger, although utilitarian, showed its breeding in similar technical innovation featuring a rear-mounted engine, forward control, optimum use of space and independent suspension with coil and rubber springing.

The basic vehicle has been developed through several variations of body style and as a platform for recoilless rifles and anti-tank guided missiles. A wide variety of optional equipment includes a power take-off, extra low (Model 700 APL) crawler gear (until the five-speed gearbox was introduced), tropical kit, snow plough and a 1500 kg (3307 lb) capacity winch.

The chassis has a central tubular backbone and the wheels are independently sprung with coil/rubber springs on swing axles incorporating step down final drive gear cases providing generous ground clearance.

In 1962 a long wheelbase model was introduced, available with a canvas top or a glass fibre cab and four rear seats and also as a fire fighting appliance. This model was 3.125 m (10 ft 3 in) long, 1.4 m (4 ft 7 in) wide and 1.74 m (5 ft 11 in) high, with a 1.8-m (5 ft 11 in) wheelbase and an unladen weight of 700 kg (1543 lb).

In military service the Haflinger serves with the armies of Austria, Indonesia, Italy, the Netherlands, Nigeria, South Africa, Switzerland and Sweden, where it has been adapted to mount the Bofors 90 mm recoilless rifle or fire Bantam ATGWs from cellular launchers.

The Steyr-Daimler-Puch Haflinger has been out of production for a decade but is still in widespread military service and beloved by off-road vehicle enthusiasts

MANUFACTURER: Steyr-Daimler-Puch AG, Graz, Austria (1959–1974)

CONFIGURATION: 4 × 4, rear-engined, open body or hard top

doors	seats	unladen weight	max load
4	1 + 3	645 kg (1422 lb)	555 kg (1224 lb)

ENGINE: Model 700 AP 2-cylinder, flat twin, air-cooled petrol developing 24 hp at 4500 rpm

TRANSMISSION: Manual

Type of clutch	single dry plate
Number of gear ratios	4 forward, 1 reverse/5 forward, 1 reverse post-1966

CHASSIS AND SUSPENSION: Unitary construction, independent suspension all round by coil and rubber springs

Fuel tank	31.5 litres (6.93 gallons)
Brakes	drums
Tyres	165 × 12
Electrical system	12V

DIMENSIONS:

swb	
Length	2.85 m (9 ft 4 in)
Width	1.4 m (4 ft 7 in)
Height	1.74 m (5 ft 8 in)
Wheelbase	1.5 m (4 ft 11 in)
Track	1.13 m (3 ft 8 in)
Turning radius	3.8 m (12 ft)
Ground clearance	0.24 m (9 in)
Fording	0.4 m (1 ft 4 in)
Gradient	65%

lwb	
Length	3.125 m (10 ft 3 in)
Width	1.4 m (4 ft 7 in)
Height	1.74 m (5 ft 8 in)
Wheelbase	1.8 m (5 ft 11 in)

PERFORMANCE:

Max speed	75 km/h (47 mph)
Operating range	400 km (248 miles)

STEYR-DAIMLER-PUCH PINZGAUER

The Haflinger's big brother, the Pinzgauer

The prototype of the Pinzgauer, the big brother to the Haflinger was produced in 1965 although series production did not begin until 1971 and a 6 × 6 version (Model 712) soon afterwards. The vehicle has a central tube chassis with swing axles and an air-cooled engine.

Optional equipment includes power take-offs and a hydraulic system to power auxiliaries including a two-tonne capacity cable winch.

TRANSMISSION:	Manual	
	Type of clutch	single dry plate
	Number of gear ratios	5 forward, 1 reverse
	Transfer box	2-speed

CHASSIS AND SUSPENSION:	Central tube chassis with twin axles. Independent suspension all round tyre coil springs, progressive rubber hollow springs and double-acting shock absorbers	
	Fuel tank	75 litres (16.49 gallons) (125 litres (27.59 gallons) optional)
	Brakes	dual circuit drum with power assist
	Steering	worm and roller
	Tyres	6.50 × 16
	Electrical system	12V

DIMENSIONS:	Length	4.175 m (13 ft 8 in)
	Width	1.76 m (5 ft 9 in)
	Height	2.045 m (6 ft 8 in)
	Wheelbase	2.2 m (7 ft 3 in)
	Track	1.44 m (4 ft 9 in)
	Turning radius	5.17 m (17 ft)
	Ground clearance	0.335 m (1 ft 1 in)
	Fording	0.7 m (2 ft 3 in)
	Gradient	100%
	Angle of approach/departure	45°/45°

MANUFACTURER:	Steyr-Daimler-Puch AG, Graz, Austria		

CONFIGURATION:	4 × 4, front-engined, open body with canvas top (type 710M), enclosed steel body (type 710K)		
	doors	**unladen weight**	**max load**
710M	4	1950 kg (4299 lb)	1000 kg (2205 lb)

ENGINE:	4-cylinder, 249 cc, air-cooled petrol, developing 67 hp at 4000 rpm	
	Torque	177 Nm at 2000 rpm
	Compression ratio	7.5:1

PERFORMANCE:	Max speed	110 km/h (68 mph)
	Fuel consumption	17 litres/100 km (77.28 gallons/62 miles)

SUBARU 1600

Subaru 1600 station wagon

Subaru found a new market niche in 1974 when they launched a four-wheel drive station wagon variant of their then current 1600 range. Since then the company has been consistently at the forefront of the dual purpose four-wheel drive market.

Interesting features are the flat four engine and innovative suspension geometry, whereas the interiors are still stuck in the somewhat tasteless mid-1970s Japanese mould.

Subaru also build a four wheel drive microbus called the Domingo. Conversions of the VW Transporter and Ford Transit as off-road crew buses were also launched in 1983–4.

MANUFACTURER:	Fuji Heavy Industries, Tokyo, Japan

CONFIGURATION:	4 × 4 saloon, hatchback, station wagon

	doors	seats	unladen weight	max load
Saloon	4	5	980 kg	420 kg
			(2160 lb)	(926 lb)
Coupé	3	5	915 kg	265 kg
			(2017 lb)	(584 lb)
Station wagon	5	5	1020 kg	455 kg
			(2249 lb)	(1003 lb)

ENGINE:	EA 71 4-cylinder, 1595 cc, water-cooled, horizontally opposed, in light alloy developing 87 hp at 5600 rpm

TRANSMISSION:	Manual with selectable 4 × 4 or 4 × 2	
	Type of clutch	single dry plate
	Number of gear ratios	4 forward, 1 reverse
	Transfer box	2-speed

CHASSIS AND SUSPENSION:	Unitary construction, independent suspension all round	
	Fuel tank	55 litres (12.1 gallons)
	Brakes	discs at front, drums at rear, power assisted
	Steering	rack and pinion, power optional
	Tyres	6.15 × 13
	Electrical system	12V

DIMENSIONS:	Saloon	
	Length	4.265 m (14 ft)
	Width	1.62 m (5 ft 4 in)
	Height	1.41 m (4 ft 7 in)
	Wheelbase	2.45 m (8 ft)
	Track	1.315 m/1.345 m (rear) (4 ft 4 in/4 ft 5 in)
	Turning radius	4.8 m (16 ft)
	Ground clearance	0.21 m (8 in)
	Hatchback	
	Length	3.995 m (13 ft 1 in)
	Width	1.62 m (5 ft 4 in)
	Height	1.415 m (4 ft 8 in)
	Wheelbase	2.37 m (7 ft 9 in)
	Track	1.315 m/1.345 m (rear) (4 ft 4 in/4 ft 5 in)
	Turning radius	4.7 m (15 ft 6 in)
	Ground clearance	0.175 m (7 in)
	Station wagon	
	Length	4.275 m (14 ft)
	Width	1.62 m (5 ft 4 in)
	Height	1.445 m (4 ft 9 in)
	Wheelbase	2.445 m (8 ft)
	Track	1.315 m/1.345 m (rear) (4 ft 4 in/4 ft 5 in)
	Turning radius	4.8 m (16 ft)
	Ground clearance	0.175 m (7 in)

PERFORMANCE:	Max speed	135 km/h (84 mph)
	Power-to-weight ratio	10.5 kg/hp (23.15 lb/hp)
	Fuel consumption	9–13 litres/100 km (1.98–2.86 gallons/62 miles)

SUBARU 1800

MANUFACTURER:	Fuji Heavy Industries, Tokyo, Japan
CONFIGURATION:	4 × 4 saloon, hatchback, station wagon
ENGINE:	EA 81 4-cylinder, 1782 cc, water-cooled, horizontally opposed, in light alloy developing 100 hp at 5600 rpm (Japan). RX version, 110 hp at 6000 rpm

TRANSMISSION:	Manual or automatic, selectable 4 × 4 or 4 × 2	
	Type of clutch	single dry plate
	Number of gear ratios	4 forward, 1 reverse
	Transfer box	2-speed (station wagon)

CHASSIS AND SUSPENSION:	Fuel tank	55 litres (12.1 gallons)
	Brakes	discs at front, drums at rear, power assisted
	Steering	rack and pinion, power assisted
	Electrical system	12V

SUBARU REX 4WD

MANUFACTURER:	Fuji Heavy Industries, Tokyo, Japan

CONFIGURATION:	4 × 4, two-door hatchback saloon		
	doors	**seats**	**unladen weight**	**max load**

doors	seats	unladen weight	max load
3	4	650 kg (1433 lb)	

ENGINE:	EK 23 2-cylinder, 544 cc, water-cooled, in-line, mounted transversely, developing 31 hp at 6000 rpm

TRANSMISSION:	Manual	
	Type of clutch	single dry plate
	Number of gear ratios	5 forward, 1 reverse

CHASSIS AND SUSPENSION:	Unitary construction	
	Fuel tank	31 litres (6.82 gallons)
	Brakes	drum
	Tyres	5.20 × 10
	Electrical system	12V

DIMENSIONS:	Length	3.195 m (10 ft 6 in)
	Width	1.395 m (4 ft 7 in)
	Height	1.35 m (4 ft 5 in)
	Wheelbase	2.255 m (7 ft 5 in)
	Track	1.22 m (4 ft)
	Ground clearance	0.175 m (7 in)

PERFORMANCE:	Max speed	110 km/h (68 mph)
	Power-to-weight ratio	20.6 kg/hp (45.41 lb/hp)
	Fuel consumption	4–9 litres/100 km (0.88–1.98 gallons/62 miles)

Top: Subaru 1800 hatchback
Right: 1800 automatic estate
Far right: The 1800 four wheel drive pick up, often seen with a purpose designed fibreglass hardtop

SUZUKI SJ410 SERIES

The ultra-lightweight and comparatively small Jimny 550 series proved the principle and Suzuki produced a development of the basic vehicle powered by a four-stroke water-cooled engine which has met with considerable marketing success worldwide. The SJ410 model has half doors with roll bar, the SJ410V is a steel bodied station wagon, the SJ410QG has a removable plastic top, the SJ410Q has canvas top and full doors, the SJ410W is a long wheelbase model with canvas top and the SJ410K is a long wheelbase pick-up with steel cab.

Four-wheel drive can be selected at will with freewheeling hubs offered as optional.

MANUFACTURER:	Suzuki Motor Co., Hamamatsu, Japan				
CONFIGURATION:	4 × 4, front-engined, open body with canvas top with half doors (SJ410), station wagon (SJ410V), removable plastic hard top (SJ410QG), open body canvas top full door (SJ410Q), open body canvas top full full door long wheelbase (SJ410W), pick-up (SJ410K), lowbody pick-up (SJ410WP)				
		doors	seats	unladen weight	max load
	SJ410	2	4	805 kg (1775 lb)	445 kg (981 lb)
	SJ410Q	2	4	815 kg (1797 lb)	430 kg (948 lb)
	SJ410V	3	4	850 kg (1874 lb)	400 kg (882 lb)
	SJ410QG	3	4	850 kg (1874 lb)	400 kg (882 lb)
	SJ410W	2	4–6	865 kg (1907 lb)	485 kg (1069 lb)
	SJ410K	2	2	860 kg (1896 lb)	490 kg (1080 lb)
	SJ410WP	2	2	850 kg (1874 lb)	500 kg (1102 lb)
ENGINE:	Suzuki 4-cylinder, 970 cc, water-cooled, petrol developing 45 hp at 5500 rpm				
	Torque	73.5 Nm at 3000 rpm			
TRANSMISSION:	Manual, selectable 4 × 2 or 4 × 4, freewheel on front hubs optional				
	Type of clutch	single dry plate			
	Number of gear ratios	4 forward, 1 reverse			
	Transfer box	2-speed			
CHASSIS AND SUSPENSION:	Channel section ladder type. Suspension by semi-elliptical leaf springs all round with double-action hydraulic shock absorbers				
	Fuel tank	40 litres (8.8 gallons)			
	Brakes	discs front, drums rear			
	Steering	ball and nut			
	Electrical system	12V			

SJ410 cutaway shows the kind of engineering packed into such a small vehicle. Leaf springs are used all round with disc brakes on front wheels only

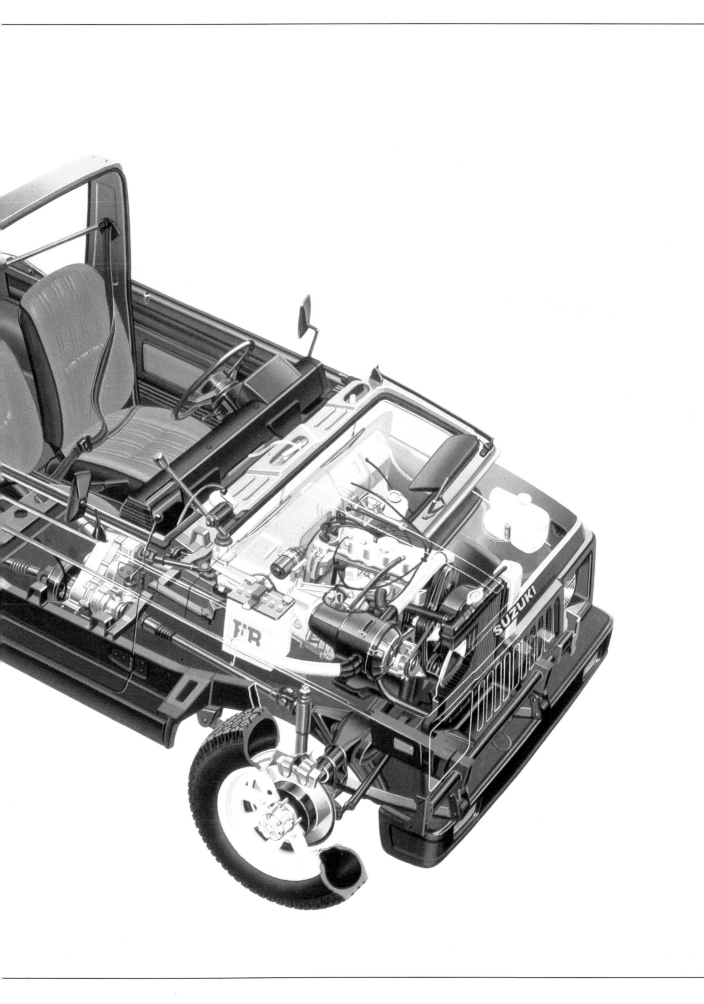

DIMENSIONS:

SJ410/SJ410Q

Length	3.41 m (11 ft 2 in)
Width	1.395 m (4 ft 7 in)
Height	1.69 m (5 ft 6 in)
Wheelbase	2.03 m (6 ft 8 in)
Track	1.21 m/1.22 m (rear) (4 ft/4 ft)
Turning radius	4.9 m (16 ft) (5.7 m (19 ft) lwb)
Ground clearance	2.4 m (7 ft 10 in)

SJ410V

Length	3.42 m (11 ft 2 in)
Width	1.395 m (4 ft 7 in)
Height	1.7 m (5 ft 7 in)
Wheelbase	2.03 m (6 ft 8 in)

SJ410QG

Length	3.41 m (11 ft 2 in)
Width	1.395 m (4 ft 7 in)
Height	1.7 m (5 ft 7 in)
Wheelbase	2.03 m (6 ft 8 in)

SJ410W

Length	3.99 m (13 ft 1 in)
Width	1.395 m (4 ft 7 in)
Height	1.83 m (6 ft)
Wheelbase	2.375 m (7 ft 9 in)

SJ410K

Length	3.89 m (12 ft 9 in)
Width	1.395 m (4 ft 7 in)
Height	1.69 m (5 ft 6 in)
Wheelbase	2.375 m (7 ft 9 in)

SJ410WP

Length	3.99 m (13 ft 1 in)
Width	1.395 m (4 ft 7 in)
Height	1.92 m (6 ft 4 in)
Wheelbase	2.375 m (7 ft 9 in)

Right: The panache of the diminutive Suzukis has earned them a worldwide following
Below: SJ 410K pick-up
Below right: SJ 410W soft-top long wheelbase
Centre right: SJ 410Q full door soft-top
Far right: SJ 410V station wagon

SUZUKI ALTO

With the Alto, Suzuki brought four-wheel drive to the sophisticated small coupé market. In essence the car embodies the well-proven engine and drive package from the SJ410 series with the Alto bodyshell and an interior which would pass as luxurious. Like the Subarus and AMC's Eagle it is aimed squarely at the 'snow-belt' market.

TRANSMISSION:	Manual, selectable 4 × 2 or 4 × 4
	Type of clutch single dry plate
	Number of gear ratios 4 forward, 1 reverse
	1) 4.1:1 2) 2.166:1 3) 1.375:1 4) 0.933:1
	Rev. 3.363:1 Final drive 5.733 front/3.272:1 rear

CHASSIS AND SUSPENSION:	Unitary construction. Independent front suspension by coil springs. Rear rigid axle with semi-elliptical leaf springs, telescopic shock absorbers all round
	Fuel tank 27 litres (5.94 gallons)
	Brakes drums all round
	Steering rack and pinion
	Tyres 5.00 × 10
	Electrical system 12V

MANUFACTURER:	Suzuki Motor Co., Hamamatsu, Japan

CONFIGURATION:	4 × 4, front-engined, hatchback saloon

	doors	seats	unladen weight
Alto	3	4	605 kg (1334 lb)

DIMENSIONS:	Length	3.19 m (10 ft 6 in)
	Width	1.39 m (4 ft 7 in)
	Height	1.33 m (4 ft 4 in)
	Wheelbase	2.15 m (7 ft 1 in)
	Track	1.21 m/1.17 m (rear) (4 ft 3 ft 10 in)
	Turning radius	4.4 m (14 ft)
	Ground clearance	0.165 m (6 in)

ENGINE:	3-cylinder, 543 cc, water-cooled petrol developing 28 hp at 6000 rpm
	Torque 41 Nm at 4000 rpm
	Compression ratio 9.5:1

PERFORMANCE:	Max speed	110 km/h (68 mph)
	Power-to-weight ratio	21.6 kg/hp (47.62 lb/hp)
	Fuel consumption	3.4 litres/100 km (0.75 gallons/62 miles)

SUZUKI JIMNY 550

The little Jimny is one of the world's smallest production four-wheel drive vehicles (that title was challenged by the Fiat Panda in 1984) and commands a wide 'fun'-following as well as a serious market.

Early models were powered by a 2-stroke engine of only 359 cc driving through a four speed transmission. The current model is powered by a three cylinder water cooled engine of 539 cc and is offered as a station wagon, soft top or semi-cab model with full metal door.

MANUFACTURER: Suzuki Motor Co., Hamamatsu, Japan

CONFIGURATION: 4 × 4, front-engined open body with canvas top, station wagon

	doors	seats	unladen weight	max load
SJ30 FK	2 (half)	4	720 kg (1587 lb)	250 kg (551 lb)
SJ30 JM	2 (full)	4	735 kg (1621 lb)	250 kg (551 lb)
SJ30 VJC	3	4	760 kg (1676 lb)	200 kg (441 lb)
SJ30 VA	3	4	750 kg (1654 lb)	200 kg (441 lb)

ENGINE: 3-cylinder, 539 cc, 2-stroke water-cooled petrol developing 28 hp at 4500 rpm
Torque   52 Nm at 3000 rpm
Compression ratio   6.5:1

TRANSMISSION: Manual with selectable 4 × 4 or 4 × 2, freewheeling front hubs optional
Type of clutch   single dry plate
Number of gear ratios   4 forward, 1 reverse
1) 3.834:1   2) 3.58:1   3) 1.542:1   4) 1:1
Rev. 4.026:1   Final drive 4.777:1
Transfer box   2-speed   3.052:1/1.741:1

CHASSIS AND SUSPENSION: Box section ladder type. Rigid axle front and rear with semi-elliptical leaf springs and telescopic shock absorbers

Fuel tank	40 litres (8.8 gallons)
Brakes	discs front, drums rear
Steering	recirculating ball
Tyres	6.00 × 16
Electrical system	12V

DIMENSIONS:

Length	3.195 m (10 ft 6 in)
Width	1.395 m (4 ft 6 in)
Height	1.69 m (5 ft 6 in) (soft top), 1.7 m (5 ft 6 in) (van)
Wheelbase	2.03 m (6 ft 7 in)
Track	1.19 m/1.12 m (rear) (3 ft 11 in/3 ft 9 in)
Turning radius	4.9 m (16 ft)
Ground clearance	0.24 m (9 in)
Gradient	75%
Angle of approach/departure	48°/30°

PERFORMANCE:

Max speed	90 km/h (56 mph)
Power-to-weight ratio	24 kg/hp (53 lb/hp)
Fuel consumption	6.3 litres/100 km (1.38 gallons/62 miles)

TOYOTA LAND CRUISER STATION WAGON

Toyota's ability to build and sell 4 × 4 vehicles has been amply demonstrated on the west coast of Australia and Central Africa where this civilised but tough station wagon holds some 80 per cent of the market. Although having little to show in the way of revolutionary engineering, the big Toyota has earned itself an excellent reputation for reliability in adverse conditions. The vehicle was extensively redesigned in the late seventies and seems set to continue as a market leader.

MANUFACTURER : Toyota Motor Company, Nagoya, Japan

CONFIGURATION 4 × 4, front-engined, station wagon, high roof line model (GX)

	doors	seats	unladen weight	max load
Station wagon	5	5–6	1895 kg (4187 lb)	820 kg (1808 lb)
Station wagon G	5	5–6	1890 kg (4167 lb)	820 kg (1808 lb)
Station wagon High Roof	5	8	1935 kg (4266 lb)	820 kg (1808 lb)

ENGINE : i) Toyota 2F 6-cylinder, 4320 cc, water-cooled petrol, developing 135 hp at 3600 rpm
Torque   29 kgm at 1800 rpm
Compression ratio   7.8:1
ii) Toyota 2H 6-cylinder, 3980 cc, water-cooled diesel, developing 103 hp at 3500 rpm
Torque   24.5 kgm at 2000 rpm
Compression ratio   19:1
iii) Toyota 3B 4-cylinder, 3431 cc, water-cooled diesel developing 90 hp at 3500 rpm
Torque   22 kgm at 2200 rpm
Compression ratio   20:1

TRANSMISSION : Manual 4-speed or 5-speed. Selectable 4 × 4 or 4 × 2 optional freewheeling front hubs
Type of clutch   single dry plate

Number of gear ratios   4 forward, 1 reverse
1) 4.843:1   2) 2.619:1   3) 1.516:1   4) 1:1
Rev. 4.843:1   Final drive 3.6:1 (4.111:1 diesel)
Number of gear ratios   5 forward, 1 reverse (G and GX models)
1) 4.843:1   2) 2.619:1   3) 1.516:1   4) 1:1
5) 0.845:1
Transfer box   2-speed   1.961:1/1:1

Toyota Land Cruiser Station Wagon cutaway shows a massive ladder frame chassis and leaf springs all round. Winch is optional

CHASSIS AND SUSPENSION: Box section ladder type with steel body. Semi-elliptical leaf springs all round with double-acting hydraulic shock absorbers

Fuel tank	90 litres (19.79 gallons)
Brakes	discs front, drums rear with optional power assist
Steering	recirculating ball
Electrical system	12V

DIMENSIONS:

Length	4.675 m (15 ft 4 in)
Width	1.8 m (5 ft 11 in)
Height	1.815 m (5 ft 11 in)
	(1.93 m (6 ft 4 in) high roof)
Wheelbase	2.73 m (8 ft 11 in)
Track	1.475 m/1.46 m (rear)
	(4 ft 10 in/4 ft 9 in)
Ground clearance	0.21 m (8 in)

TOYOTA BLIZZARD

The very attractive Blizzard is so far sold only in Japanese home markets but represents the ultimate new generation replacement for the Land Cruiser series, very much in the mould of the Land-Rover 90 and 110. The Blizzard has boxy purposeful styling and is sold either as a station wagon or full length soft top. While the engineering remains true to Land Cruiser practice – a rugged ladder frame chassis and leaf springs front and rear, technical refinements include 3-stage shock absorbers with selectable hard or soft ride.

MANUFACTURER:	Toyota Motor Company, Nagoya, Japan

CONFIGURATION: 4 × 4, front-engined, open body with canvas top, hard top, station wagon

	doors	seats	unladen weight	max load
Open body	2	6	1205 kg (2657 lb)	355 kg (783 lb)
Station wagon	3	4	1255 kg (2767 lb)	400 kg (882 lb)

ENGINE: 4-cylinder, 2188 cc, water-cooled petrol developing 72 hp at 4200 rpm
Torque	142 Nm at 2400 rpm
Compression ratio	21.5:1

TRANSMISSION: Manual, 4- or 5-speed box, optional differential lock
Number of gear ratios i) 4 forward, 1 reverse
                                         ii) 5 forward, 1 reverse
i) 1) 3.717:1 2) 2.504:1 3) 1.513:1 4) 1:1
Rev. 4.434:1 Final drive 3.909:1
ii) 1) 3.717:1 2) 2.177:1 3) 1.513:1 4) 1:1
5) 0.876:1 Rev. 4.434:1 Final drive 3.909:1
Transfer box   2-speed   1.307:1/2.407:1

CHASSIS AND SUSPENSION: Ladder frame type chassis. Rigid front axles front and rear with semi-elliptical leaf springs and telescopic shock absorbers

Fuel tank	48 litres (10.56 gallons)
Brakes	front discs, rear drums, servo
Steering	recirculating ball
Tyres	6.00 × 16
Electrical system	12V

DIMENSIONS:
Length	3.52 m (11 ft 7 in)
Width	1.46 m (4 ft 9 in)
Height	1.87 m (6 ft 1 in)
Wheelbase	2.025 m (6 ft 8 in)
Track	1.2 m (3 ft 11 in)
Turning radius	5.15 m (17 ft)
Ground clearance	0.215 m (8 in)

PERFORMANCE:
Max speed	120 km/h (75 mph)
Power-to-weight ratio	16.7 kg/hp (36.82 lb/hp)
Fuel consumption	9 litres/100 km (1.98 gallons/62 miles)

The Blizzard, Toyota's new generation off-road vehicle shows strong signs of its Land Cruiser parentage in its engineering

TOYOTA TERCEL

Launched in 1981, the Tercel is a luxurious estate car with an unusual transmission rather than an off-road vehicle proper. There are five forward and an 'extra low' gear which can be engaged when four-wheel drive is selected. The body is unitary construction with coil springs all round.

MANUFACTURER:	Toyota Motor Corporation, Nagoya, Japan			
CONFIGURATION:	4 × 4 station wagon			
	doors	seats	unladen weight	max load
	5	5	1015 kg	450 kg
			(2238 lb)	(992 lb)
ENGINE:	4-cylinder 1453 cc, water-cooled in-line developing 71 hp at 5600 rpm (US, 62 hp at 4800 rpm)			
TRANSMISSION:	Manual with selectable 4 × 2 or automatic			
	Type of clutch	single dry plate		
	Number of gear ratios	5 forward, 1 reverse		
	Transfer box	2-speed		
CHASSIS AND SUSPENSION:	Unitary construction			
	Fuel tank	50 litres (11 gallons)		
	Brakes	power assisted discs at front, drums at rear		
	Steering	rear rack and pinion		
	Electrical system	12V		
DIMENSIONS:	Length	4.31 m (14 ft 1 in)		
	Width	1.615 m (5 ft 4 in)		
	Height	1.51 m (5 ft)		
	Wheelbase	2.43 m (8 ft)		
	Track	1.38 m/1.35 m (rear) (4 ft 6 in/4 ft 6 in)		
	Turning radius	5.2 m (17 ft)		
	Ground clearance	0.175 m (7 in)		
PERFORMANCE:	Max speed	155 km/h (96 mph)		
	Power-to-weight ratio	11.7 kg/hp (25.8 lb/hp)		
	Fuel consumption	5.6–8.6 litres/100 km (1.23–1.9 gallons/62 miles)		

The Tercel is aimed squarely at the dual-purpose off-road market; rather than the rough and tough conditions which its fellow models in the Toyota line-up might encounter

TOYOTA BANDEIRANTE

Toyota began building Land Cruisers in Brazil with an assembly plant in Sau Paulo in the late 1950s. The Land Cruiser range is marketed as the 'Bandeirante' and the range of station wagon, soft-top, hard-top and pick-up are all powered by a four-cylinder Mercedes-Benz diesel.

MANUFACTURER: Toyota do Brasil, São Bernardo, Do Campo, Brazil

CONFIGURATION: 4 × 4, front-engined, station wagon on two wheel bases

	doors	seats	unladen weight	max load
swb	3	5	1580 kg (3483 lb)	1420 kg (3130 lb)
lwb	3	7	1760 kg (3880 lb)	950 kg (2094 lb)

ENGINE: Mercedes-Benz OM314, 5784 cc, water-cooled diesel developing 85 hp at 2800 rpm
Torque 235 Nm at 1800 rpm
Compression ratio 17:1

TRANSMISSION: Manual, selectable 4 ×2 or 4 ×4
Type of clutch single dry plate
Number of gear ratios 4 forward, 1 reverse
1) 4.925:1 2) 2.643:1 3) 1.519:1 4) 1:1
Rev. 4.925:1 Final drive 3.7:1
Transfer box 2-speed 1.992:1/1:1

CHASSIS AND SUSPENSION: Channel section ladder type chassis. All steel body. Semi-elliptical leaf springs front and rear with double-acting hydraulic shock absorbers

Fuel tank	52 litres (11.43 gallons)
Brakes	drums all round with power assist
Steering	recirculating ball
Tyres	7.50 ×16
Electrical system	12V

DIMENSIONS:
swb	
Length	3.915 (12 ft 10 in)
Width	1.665 m (5 ft 5 in)
Height	1.945 m (6 ft 4 in)
Wheelbase	2.285 m (7 ft 6 in)
Track	1.415 m/1.41 m (rear) (4 ft 8 in/4 ft 7 in)
Turning radius	5.3 m (17 ft)
Ground clearance	0.21 (8 in)
lwb	
Length	4.3 m (14 ft 1 in)
Wheelbase	2.75 m (9 ft)
Turning radius	5.5 m (18 ft)

PERFORMANCE:
Max speed	105 km/h (65 mph)
Power-to-weight ratio	18.6 kg/hp (41 lb/hp)
Fuel consumption	9–10 litres/100 km (1.97–2.19 gallons/62 miles)

TOYOTA LAND CRUISER SERIES

One of the symbols of the post war Japanese car industry's rebirth and then conquest of world markets, the Land Cruiser range has given European manufacturers such as Land Rover a tough run for their money in Asian and African markets for almost three decades.

Toyota began in 1951 with the Jeep lookalike model BJ but by the late 1950s a tough and businesslike vehicle had evolved and found the world at its feet. The Land Cruiser range has been extensively technically developed but remains true to the basic principles of ladder frame chassis and leaf-sprung live axles all round. Six basic models are in production on two wheelbases and are used as military vehicles by many armed forces round the world.

MANUFACTURER: Toyota Motor Corporation, Nagoya, Japan

CONFIGURATION: 4 × 4, front-engined, open body with vinyl top on three wheelbases, pick-up station wagon on two wheelbases, long wheelbase

	doors	seats	unladen weight	max load
swb open body	2	2–7	1680 kg (3704 lb)	615 kg (1356 lb)
lwb open body	2–8	2–8	1740 kg (3836 lb)	700 kg (1543 lb)
super lwb open body	2	2–10	1865 kg (4111 lb)	1170 kg (2579 lb)
swb hard top	3	2–6	1715 kg (3781 lb)	625 kg (1378 lb)
super lwb hard top	3	2–10	1925 kg (4244 lb)	1100 kg (2425 lb)
pick-up	2	2	1860 kg (4101 lb)	1175 kg (2590 lb)

(weights are for petrol engine with 4-speed transmission)

ENGINE:
i) Toyota 2F 6-cylinder, 4230 cc, water-cooled petrol developing 135 hp at 3600 rpm
Torque 29 kg m at 1800 rpm
Compression ratio 7.8:1
(available on all models)
ii) Toyota 2H 6-cylinder, 3980 cc, water-cooled diesel developing 103 hp at 3500 rpm
Torque 24.5 kg m at 2000 rpm
Compression ratio 19:1
(available on super lwb pick-up and hard top)
iii) Toyota 3B 4-cylinder, 3431 cc, water-cooled diesel developing 90 hp at 3500 rpm
Torque 22 kg m at 2200 rpm
Compression ratio 20:1
(available on all models except long wheelbase vinyl tops)
iv) Toyota B 4-cylinder, 2977 cc, water-cooled diesel developing 80 hp at 3600 rpm
Torque 19.5 kg m at 2200 rpm
Compression ratio 21:1

TRANSMISSION:	Manual, selectable 4 × 4 or 4 × 2, optional freewheeling front hubs

Type of clutch   single dry plate
Number of gear ratios   i) 3 forward, 2 reverse
1) 2.757:1   2) 1.691:1   3) 1:1   Rev. 3.676:1
Transfer box   2-speed   2.277:1/1:1
                     ii) 4 forward, 1 reverse
1) 4.843:1   2) 2.619:1   3) 1.516:1   4) 1:1
Rev. 4.843:1
Final drive 3.7:1 (petrol), 4.111:1 (diesel)

CHASSIS AND SUSPENSION: Channel section ladder type chassis. All steel body. Semi-elliptical leaf springs front and rear with double-acting hydraulic shock absorbers

Fuel tank	85 litres (18.7 gallons)
Brakes	drums all round
Steering	recirculating ball
Tyres	7.50 ×15
Electrical system	12V

DIMENSIONS:

swb
Length	3.915 m (12 ft 10 in)
Width	1.665 m (5 ft 5 in)
Height	1.945 m (6 ft 5 in)
Wheelbase	2.285 m (7 ft 6 in)
Track	1.415 m/1.4 m (rear) (4 ft 8 in/4 ft 7 in)
Turning radius	5.3 m (17 ft)
Ground clearance	0.21 m (8 in)

lwb
Length	4.275 m (14 ft)
Wheelbase	2.43 m (8 ft)
Track	1.415 m/1.41 m (rear) (4 ft 8 in/4 ft 7 in)
Turning radius	5.5 m (18 ft)
Ground clearance	0.21 m (8 in)

super lwb
Length	4.995 m (16 ft 5 in)
Height	2.035 m (6 ft 8 in) (hard top)
Wheelbase	2.95 m (9 ft 8 in)
Turning radius	6.5 m (21 ft)
Ground clearance	0.225 m (9 in)

Below: Land Cruiser pick-up. Top right: Standard wheelbase hard top. Right: Super long wheelbase soft top.

TOYOTA HILUX

The Hilux light truck range comes in two- and four-wheel drive varieties on two wheelbases including a five-seat four-door crew cab model with a 2-litre petrol or 2.5-litre diesel engine. Freewheeling front hubs are standard.

MANUFACTURER:	Toyota Motor Corporation, Nagoya, Japan

CONFIGURATION: 4 × 4, front-engined, pick-up, crew cab pick-up

	doors	seats	unladen weight	max load
swb	2	2	1300 kg (2866 lb)	1180 kg (2601 lb)
lwb	2	2	1320 kg (2910 lb)	1160 kg (2557 lb)
lwb with crew cab	4	5	1370 kg (3020 lb)	1110 kg (2447 lb)

(diesel is c. 100 kg (220 lb) heavier)

ENGINE:
i) Toyota 3YF 4-cylinder, 1998 cc, water-cooled developing 88 bhp at 4600 rpm
Torque 157 Nm at 3000 rpm
ii) Toyota 2L 4-cylinder, 2446 cc, water-cooled diesel developing 74 bhp at 4000 rpm
Torque 146 Nm at 220 rpm

TRANSMISSION:
Manual
Type of clutch — single dry plate
Number of gear ratios — 4 forward, 1 reverse
1) 3.939:1 2) 2.333:1 3) 1.452:1 4) 1:1
Rev. 4.744:1   Final drive 4.875:1
Transfer box — 2-speed 2.277:1/1:1

CHASSIS AND SUSPENSION:
Box section ladder type. Semi-elliptical leaf springs all round with hydraulic shock absorbers

Fuel tank	65 litres (14.29 gallons)
Brakes	drums all round, front discs optional
Steering	ball nut
Tyres	7.00 × 15
Electrical system	12V

DIMENSIONS:

swb
Length	4.435 m (14 ft 7 in)
Width	1.69 m (5 ft 6 in)
Height	1.76 m (5 ft 9 in)
Wheelbase	2.605 m (8 ft 6 in)
Track	1.42 m/1.4 m (rear) (4 ft 8 in/4 ft 7 in)
Turning radius	5.9 m (19 ft)
Ground clearance	0.22 m (9 in)

lwb
Length	4.73 m (15 ft 6 in)
Height	1.805 m (5 ft 11 in) (crew cab)
Wheelbase	2.84 m (9 ft 4 in)

Top: Toyota Hilux, a very popular four wheel drive pick up worldwide
Right: The five seat, four-door Hilux crew cab provides a very versatile working off road vehicle

UAZ-469B

Italian registered UAZ-469B

Development of the UAZ-469B dates from 1960 when it was first tested as a replacement for the GAZ-69 light vehicle for service with the Soviet Army. The original pilot model designated UAZ-460B was never put into production but a developed version, the UAZ-469B entered military service in 1973 and is now in widespread use with the armed forces of the Warsaw Pact including the Soviet Union, East Germany, Hungary and Poland, and has been exported to Iraq, Iran and Syria with production continuing. A civil version is marketed in the West as the 'Tundra' with a Peugeot diesel or Fiat petrol engine.

The military vehicle is of the normal Jeep-type layout with an all-steel body and separate chassis displaying typical Soviet 1950s-vintage front-end styling. Normal load is two crew plus 600 kg (1323 lb) of cargo or 7 crew plus 100 kg (220 lb) of cargo. Variants include hard top versions, a four-stretcher ambulance and various specialised van-type bodies.

ENGINE:	ZMZ-451M, water-cooled 2.4-litre, 4-cylinder petrol developing 75 hp at 4000 rpm	
TRANSMISSION:	Manual	
	Type of clutch	single dry plate
	Number of gear ratios	4 forward, 1 reverse
	Transfer box	2-speed
CHASSIS AND SUSPENSION:	Separate ladder frame type chassis. Longitudinal semi-elliptical springs with double-acting shock absorbers on both axles	
	Fuel tank	78 litres (17.16 gallons) (2 × 39 litres (2 × 8.58 gallons)
	Brakes	hydraulic drum on all wheels, mechanical parking
	Tyres	4 and 1 spare, 8.40 × 15
	Electrical system	12V
DIMENSIONS:	Length	4.025 m (13 ft 2 in)
	Width	1.78 m (5 ft 10 in)
	Height	2.015 m (6 ft 7 in)
	Wheelbase	2.38 m (7 ft 10 in)
	Track	1.422 m (4 ft 8 in)
	Turning radius	6.5 m (21 ft)
	Ground clearance	0.22 m (9 in)
	Fording	0.7 m (2 ft 4 in)
	Gradient	62%
	Angle of approach/departure	52°/42°
PERFORMANCE:	Max speed	100 km/h (62 mph)
	Fuel consumption	10.6 litres/100 km road (2.33 gallons/62 miles), 39 litres/100 km cross-country (8.58 gallons/62 miles)

MANUFACTURER:	Ul'yanovsk Motor Vehicle Plant, USSR

CONFIGURATION:	4 × 4, front-engined, open body with canvas or removable hard top, folding screen, removable door tops

	doors	seats	unladen weight	max load
UAZ-469B	4	7	1540 kg (3395 lb)	600 kg (1323 lb)

UMM DAKARY

Marketed variously as the Transcat and Dakary, this Portuguese-built vehicle is aimed at a basic utility market which other manufacturers have priced themselves away from. It has a rugged steel tube chassis, heavy-duty leaf springs front and rear. The station wagon and hard top pick-up are powered by Indenor or Peugeot diesel engines.

The Portuguese-built Dakary provides a basic vehicle which meets needs that more sophisticated European products may not

MANUFACTURER: Uniao Metalo Mecanica, Lisbon, Portugal

CONFIGURATION: 4 × 4, front-engined, open body with canvas top, hard top, or station wagon

	doors	seats	unladen weight	max load
Hard top	2	3	1650 kg (3638 lb)	950 kg (2094 lb)

ENGINE: i) Indenor 4-cylinder, 2122 cc, water-cooled diesel developing 65 hp at 4500 rpm
Torque 121 Nm at 2000 rpm
Compression ratio 22.8:1
ii) Indenor XD2P 4-cylinder, 2304 cc, water-cooled diesel developing 67 hp at 4500 rpm
Torque 134 Nm at 2000 rpm
Compression ratio 22.2:1
iii) Peugeot, 1971 cc, water-cooled petrol developing 87 hp at 5000 rpm
Torque 162 Nm at 2500 rpm
Compression ratio 8:1

TRANSMISSION: Manual
Type of clutch single dry plate
Number of gear ratios 4 forward, 1 reverse
1) 3.73:1 2) 2.194:1 3) 1.408:1 4) 1:1
Rev. 4.9:1 Final drive 5.375:1
Transfer box 2-speed 2.026:1/1:1

CHASSIS AND SUSPENSION: Box section ladder type with steel body. Semi-elliptical leaf springs all round with gas-filled, double-acting telescopic shock absorbers

Fuel tank 67 litres (14.73 gallons)
Brakes drums all round
Steering worm and roller
Tyres 7.00 × 16
Electrical system 12V

DIMENSIONS:
Length 3.85 m (12 ft 7 in)
Width 1.57 m (5 ft 2 in)
Height 1.98 m (6 ft 6 in)
Wheelbase 2.54 m (8 ft 4 in)
Track 1.34 m/1.27 m (rear) (4 ft 5 in/4 ft 2 in)
Turning radius 5.25 m (17 ft)
Ground clearance 0.23 m (9 in)

PERFORMANCE:
Max speed 120 km/h (75 mph)
Power-to-weight ratio
Fuel consumption 9–15 litres/100 km (1.97–3.29 gallons/62 miles)

VEB SACHSENRING P3 and P2M

P3

East Germany was the only Warsaw Pact country to manufacture its own 4 × 4 light vehicles in any quantity, the Hungarian Csepel 130 light truck being manufactured only in small numbers, otherwise standardised Soviet vehicles proliferated.

The East German industry did not get off to an auspicious start – the P2M which was in production at Zwickau from 1955–62 was not an altogether successful design with poor towing qualities and a tendency to overheat. The vehicle's layout with a four-door *Kübel* body had excessive front overhang and the suspension system with transverse torsion bars produced a different wheelbase right and left. (L/R 2.85 m (7 ft 6 in)/2.215 m (7 ft 3 in).)

The P2M ceased manufacture in 1962 and has been replaced in most units of the Volksarmee by the later P3 or by Soviet-made UAZ-469Bs.

The P3 has a conventional layout but has a number of improvements in engine, transmission, suspension and body configuration over the earlier vehicle. There are doors for driver and front seat passenger and a hinged single door at the rear. The windscreen folds flat and a canvas tilt can be erected.

An amphibious vehicle designated P2MS was developed from the original vehicle, somewhat resembling a larger version of the wartime VW 166 *Schimmwagen* but plans to produce an amphibious model of the P3 did not go beyond the design stage.

The Zwickau factory – the VEB Sachsenring Automobilwerke (VEB stands for *Volkseigener Betriebe* – people's enterprises) was originally the Horch plant of the Auto Union combine.

MANUFACTURER:	Veb Sachsenring, Zwickau, German Democratic Republic		
CONFIGURATION:	4 × 4, front-engined, open body with canvas top		
	doors	seats	unladen weight	max load
	3	8	1860 kg (4100 lb)	700 kg (1543 lb)
ENGINE:	OM-635/L, 6-cylinder, 2407 cc, water-cooled petrol developing 75 hp at 3750 rpm		
TRANSMISSION:	Manual, differential locks front and rear		
	Type of clutch	single dry plate	
	Number of gear ratios	4 forward, 1 reverse + overdrive	
	Transfer box	2-speed	
CHASSIS AND SUSPENSION:	Ladder frame type. Independent suspension all round by torsion bar		
	Fuel tank	104 litres (22.88 gallons)	
	Brakes	drums	
	Tyres	7.50 × 16	
	Electrical system	12V	
DIMENSIONS:	Length	3.71 m (12 ft 2 in)	
	Width	1.95 m (6 ft 5 in)	
	Height	1.95 m (6 ft 5 in)	
	Wheelbase	2.4 m (7 ft 10 in)	
	Track	1.42 m/1.4 m (rear) (4 ft 8 in/4 ft 8 in)	
	Ground clearance	0.33 m (1 ft)	
	Gradient	60%	
PERFORMANCE:	Max speed	95 km/h (59 mph)	
	Fuel consumption	24 litres/100 km (5.28 gallons/62 miles)	

P2M

MANUFACTURER:	Veb Sachsenring, Zwickau, German Democratic Republic

CONFIGURATION:	4 × 4, front-engined, open body with canvas top

doors	seats	unladen weight	max load
4	4	1770 kg (3902 lb)	400 kg (882 lb)

ENGINE:	OM 6/35 4-cylinder, water-cooled petrol, developing 65 hp at 3500 rpm

TRANSMISSION:	Manual	
	Type of clutch	single dry plate
	Number of gear ratios	4 forward, 1 reverse
	Transfer box	2-speed

CHASSIS AND SUSPENSION:	Independent suspension all round by torsion bar	
	Fuel tank	100 litres (22 gallons)
	Brakes	drum
	Tyres	6.50 × 16
	Electrical system	12V

DIMENSIONS:	Length	3.755 m (12 ft 4 in)
	Width	1.685 m (5 ft 6 in)
	Height	1.835 m (6 ft)
	Wheelbase	2.215 m/2.285 m (right/left) (7 ft 3 in/7 ft 6 in)
	Track	1.4 m (4 ft 7 in)
	Ground clearance	0.3 m (1 ft)
	Fording	0.55 m (1 ft 10 in)

VOLVO L3304

Volvo L3304

In production from 1963–65 with the Swedish Army the only customer, the Volvo Model L3304 uses many mechanical components of the Laplander truck but with a cut-down open body with distinct roll-over frame as a reconnaissance vehicle and light weapons platform. In the anti-tank role the vehicle has been armed with a Bofors 90 mm recoilless rifle with a travelling lock for the weapon's barrel on the engine decking.

MANUFACTURER:	AB Volvo, Goteborg, Sweden			
CONFIGURATION:	4 × 4, front-engined, open body			
		doors	seats	unladen weight	max load
	L3304	–	4	1570 kg (3461 lb)	630 kg (1389 lb)
ENGINE:	Volvo B18A 4-cylinder, petrol developing 68 bhp			
TRANSMISSION:	Manual			
	Type of clutch	single dry plate		
	Number of gear ratios	4 forward, 1 reverse		
	Transfer box	2-speed		
CHASSIS AND SUSPENSION:	Box section ladder type. Semi-elliptical leaf springs all round with progressive auxiliary rubber springs and double-acting hydraulic telescopic shock absorbers			
	Fuel tank	46 litres (10.1 gallons)		
	Brakes	hydraulic		
	Steering	cam and roller		
	Tyres	8.90 × 16		
	Electrical system	12V		
DIMENSIONS:	Length	4.4 m (14 ft 5 in)		
	Width	1.7 m (5 ft 7 in)		
	Height	1.5 m (4 ft 11 in)		
	Wheelbase	2.1 m (6 ft 10 in)		
	Track	1.34 m (4 ft 5 in)		
	Turning radius	5.7 m (18 ft 8 in)		
	Ground clearance	0.285 m (11 in)		
	Fording	0.8 m (2 ft 7 in)		
	Gradient	60%		
	Angle of approach/departure	35°/32°		

The VW Iltis is built by Bombardier in Canada for the Canadian Army

VW ILTIS

In contrast to the armed forces of the Warsaw Pact which employ rigidly standardised equipment, NATO armies still manufacture and use a huge range of equipment from rifles to tank transporters with the imperative to protect national industries perhaps greater than military utility. Even brave attempts to standardise a common light vehicle have only got so far, with the VW Iltis as one result of the process.

The requirement by the West German Army for a replacement for the Auto Union Munga was announced in 1964, then in a flurry of inter-NATO technical co-operation the project was expanded into the so-called 'NATO-Jeep' with France and Italy joining in. However, national interest and technical over-sophistication conspired eventually to kill the project.

The requirement was for an amphibious 4 × 4 cross-country vehicle to carry 500 kg. Two consortia entered prototypes, Saviem/Fiat/MAN and Bussing/Hotchkiss/Lancia. MBB and Glass/BMW also built prototypes with forward control and open, punt-like hulls.

When France withdrew in 1976 the project collapsed but West Germany continued with its Munga replacement project, dropping the amphibious requirement. Mercedes-Benz entered their G-wagen prototype (which, built by Peugeot, ironically won the French Army's new generation light vehicle contest) and Volkswagen their 'Iltis' using some mechanical components from VW and Audi passenger vehicles.

After troop trials in 1977 the VW Iltis began production in 1978 to meet a total West German Army requirement for 8800 vehicles. Meanwhile the vehicle was entered by Citroën under the designation C44 in the French Army competition but found more success in Canada where it is built under licence by Bombardier. The Quebec factory also secured marketing rights for civil versions of the vehicle worldwide.

Variants include ambulance, artillery survey, command and communications and land-line layer plus Milan ATGW anti-tank vehicle.

MANUFACTURER:	VW, Wolfsburg, West Germany		
CONFIGURATION:	4 × 4, front-engined, open body with PVC top		
	doors **seats** **unladen weight** **max load**		
	Iltis — 4 1550 kg 500 kg		
	(3417 lb) (1102 lb)		
ENGINE:	4-cylinder, 1714 cc, water-cooled petrol developing 75 bhp at 5000 rpm		
	Torque 135 Nm at 2800 rpm		
	Compression ratio 8.2:1		
TRANSMISSION:	Manual, selectable 4 × 2 or 4 × 4, optional differential lock		
	Type of clutch single dry plate		
	Number of gear ratios 5 forward, 1 reverse		
	Low 7.318:1 1) 3.909:1 2) 2.227:1 3) 1.458:1		
	Rev. 7.318:1 Final drive 5.286:1		
	Transfer box 2-speed		
CHASSIS AND SUSPENSION:	Ladder type with all steel body. Semi-elliptical leaf springs all round with double-acting shock absorbers		
	Fuel tank 85 litres (18.7 gallons)		
	Brakes drums all round		
	Steering rack and pinion		
	Tyres 6.50 × R16		
	Electrical system 12V		
DIMENSIONS:	Length 3.887 m (12 ft 9 in)		
	Width 1.52 m (5 ft)		
	Height 1.837 m (6 ft)		
	Wheelbase 2.017 m (6 ft 7 in)		
	Track 1.23 m/1.26 m (rear)		
	(4 ft/4 ft 2 in)		
	Turning radius 5.5 m (18 ft)		
	Ground clearance 0.225 m (9 in)		
	Fording 0.6 m (2 ft)		
	Gradient 77%		
	Angle of approach/departure 41°/32°		
PERFORMANCE:	Max speed 130 km/h (81 mph)		

Top: Volkswagen built a limited number of the Iltis for the civil market in 1979–80
Right: The Bombardier built version with full weather equipment

VW PASSAT TETRA

Launched in 1983, the VW Passat Tetra is Volkswagen's foray into the field of on-road 4 × 4 following in the path of its upmarket corporate stablemate the Audi Quattro and VW's own brief excursion into off-road 4 × 4 with the civil Iltis.

The five-cylinder 2-litre fuel-injected engine delivers 115 bhp at 5400 rpm driving through a five-speed gearbox and permanent four-wheel drive. Instead of the torsion beam trailing-arm rear axle of the standard Passat, the Tetra features independent wishbones with suspension struts. Power steering and disc brakes all round are standard.

MANUFACTURER:	VW, Wolfsburg, West Germany

CONFIGURATION: 4 × 4, front-engined, station wagon

doors	seats	unladen weight	max load
5	5	1310 kg (2888 lb)	510 kg (1124 lb)

ENGINE: 5-cylinder, 1994 cc, water-cooled petrol developing 115 bhp at 5400 rpm

Torque	165 Nm at 3200 rpm
Compression ratio	10:1

TRANSMISSION: Manual

Type of clutch	single dry plate
Number of gear ratios	5 forward, 1 reverse

CHASSIS AND SUSPENSION: Unitary construction

Fuel tank	70 litres (15.39 gallons)
Brakes	discs all round
Tyres	6 × 14
Electrical system	12V

DIMENSIONS:

Length	4.435 m (14 ft 7 in)
Width	1.72 m (5 ft 8 in)
Height	1.4 m (4 ft 7 in)
Wheelbase	2.55 m (8 ft 4 in)
Track	1.4 m (4 ft 7 in)
Turning radius	5.35 m (17 ft 6 in)
Ground clearance	0.12 m (5 in)

PERFORMANCE:

Max speed	182 km/h (113 mph)
Power-to-weight ratio	11.4 kg/hp (25 lb/hp)
Fuel consumption	6.8–11.8 litres/100 km (1.5–2.6 gallons/62 miles)

Launched in 1983, the VW Tetra variant propels the already popular Passat Break into the dual purpose off road and snowbelt market as well as ensuring extra safety on the autobahn at high speed

INDEX

MANUFACTURERS

ALFA ROMEO
Alfa Romeo S.p.A., via Gattamelata 45, Milan, Italy

AMC
American Motors Corporation, Car Division, 14250
Plymouth Rd, Detroit, Michigan, 48232, USA

ATW
Auto-Montan-Werke, Vertriebsgesellschaft mbH,
Westendstrasse 58–62, Paul-Ehrlich-Haus, Postfach
174294, 6000 Frankfurt/Main, Germany

AUDI
Audi NSU Auto Union AG, 8070 Ingolstadt, Germany

BEIJING JEEP CORPORATION
Chuiyangliu Chaoyang District, Beijing, China

BOMBARDIER INC.
Valcourt, Quebec, Canada, JOE 2LO

BRAVIA
Sociedade Luso-Braziliera de Viaturas e Equipamentos,
SARL, Avenue Duarte Pachecho, 21–5, Lisbon,
Portugal

CHEVROLET
Chevrolet Motor Division, Engineering Centre, 30003
Van Dyke, Warren, Michigan, USA

CITROËN
Automobiles Citroën, 62, bld Victor-Hugo, F-92208
Neuilly-sur-Seine, France

COLT
Mitsubishi Heavy Industries Ltd., 10, 2-chome
Marunouchi, Chiyoda-ku, Tokyo, Japan

COURNIL (see SIMI)

CROCO
Croco Ltd., CH-8001 Zurich, Bahnhofplatz 3,
Switzerland

DAIHATSU
Daihatsu Kogyo Co., Ltd., 1 Daihatsu-Cho, Ikeda City,
Osako, Prefecture Japan

DANGEL
Automobiles Dangel, BP 01-F68780 Sentheim, France

DATSUN (see Nissan)

DELTA
Delta Motor Corporation, PO Box 305, MCC, Makati,
Metro Manila 3117, Phillippines

DODGE
Dodge Division, Chrysler Corporation, Detroit,
Michigan 48231, USA

FIAT
Fiat SA, Corso Marconi 10, 10125 Torino, Italy

FORD USA
Ford Motor Company, P.O. Box 2053, Dearborn,
Michigan, USA

FORD BRASIL
Ford Brasil S.A., Av. Rudge Ramos, 1501 Sao Bernado
do Campo, Caixa Postal 8610, Sao Paulo, Brasil

GLENFROME
Glenfrome Engineering Ltd., Imperial Works, Hudds
Vale Rd, St George, Bristol, BS5 7HY, UK

ISUZU
Isuzu Motors Ltd., 22.10 Minami-oi 6-chome,
Shingawa-ku, Tokyo, Japan

JEEP
Jeep Corporation, American Centre, 27777 Franklin
Rd, Southfield, Michigan 48034, USA

JEG
QT Engenharia e Equipamentos LTDA, Rua des
Orquideas 475, Sao Bernado do Campo, Brasil

ACKNOWLEDGEMENTS

Campbell Rawkins would like to thank the following for supplying the photographs used in this book –

Front Cover: Rich Johnson, Pages 2–3: Rich Johnson, 7: Rich Johnson, 12: Imperial War Museum, 14: Imperial War Museum, 15: CC, 15: Imperial War Museum, 18 (from top): Nissan, British Motor Industry Heritage Trust, British Motor Industry Heritage Trust, 19 (all pictures): Jeep Corporation, 22: Ford (USA), 26: Lancia, 30: Pininfarina, 32: AMC, 33: Dacia UK, 34: Bart Vanderveen, 35: ATW, 38: VAG, 40: Beijing Jeep Corporation, 41: Chevrolet, 42: Chevrolet, 44: Citroën, 45: Citroën, 46: Citroën, 47: Croco, 48: Julian McNamara, 51: Dodge, 53: Engesa, 54: Fiat, 55: Fiat, 58–59: Ford (USA), 60: Ford (USA), 61: AM General, 64: Bart Vanderveen, 69: AMC, 70: AMC, 72: AMC, 73: AMC, 74: Rich Johnson, 76: AMC, 77: AMC, 78–79: Julian McNamara, 81 (top): British Aerospace/TRH, 83: Julian McNamara, 86–87 (all pictures): Land Rover, 88: British Motor Industry Heritage Trust, 91 (all pictures): The Research House, 93 (top): Scottorn Trailers, 93 (below): Glenfrome

LAMBORGHINI
Nuova Automonil Ferrucio Lamborghini S.p.A., via Modena 12, 40019 Sat-Agata Bolognese, Bologna, Italy

LANCIA
Lancia & Co., Fabbrica Automobil S.p.A., via Vincenzo Lancia 27, 10141 Torino, Italy

LADA
Autoexport, 14 Volkhonka St, 119902, Moscow, USSR

LAND-ROVER
Land-Rover Ltd., Military Products, Lode Lane, Solihull, West Midlands B92 8NW, UK

LOHR
Strasbourg 67980, Hangenbieten, France

LuAZ
Lutsk Motor Vehicle Plant, Ukraine, USSR

MERCEDES-BENZ
Daimler-Benz AG, Stuttgart-Unterturkheim, Germany

MITSUBISHI
Mitsubishi Heavy Industries Ltd., 10,2-chome Marunouchi, Chiyoda-ku, Tokyo, Japan

NISSAN
Nissan Motors Co, Ltd., 7,6-chome, Ginza-Higashi, Chuo-ku, Tokyo, Japan

PEUGEOT
Societé Anonyme des Automobiles Peugeot, Sochaux, France

PININFARINA
Industrie Pininfarina, Via Lesna 78/80, 10095 Grugliasco (TO), Italy

PONCIN
Vehicules Poncin S.A. Z.I. de Tournes-Cliron, 08540 Tournes

PORTARO
Sociedade Electro-Mecanica de Automoveis LDA, Rua Nova de S. Mamede, 74–8 Lisbon, Portugal

RENAULT
Regie Nationale des Usines Renault, Billancourt (Seine), France

SBARRO
ACA Atelier de Construction Automobile, 1411 Les Tuileries-de-Grandson, Switzerland

SCOTTORN TRAILERS
Scottorn Trailers Ltd., Chartridge, Chesham, Bucks, HP5 2SH, UK

SIMI
Societé Internationale de Materiels Industriels, 42260 St-Germain Laval, France

STEYR-DAIMLER-PUCH
Steyr-Daimler-Puch AG, 8011 Graz, Austria

SUBARU
Fuji Heavy Industries Ltd., Subaru Bldg., Tsunohazu, Shinju-ku Tokyo, Japan

SUZUKI
Suzuki Motor Co. Ltd., P.O. Box 116, Hamamatsu, Japan

TOYOTA
Toyota Motor Co. Ltd., Toyota-shi, Aichi-ken, Japan

UAZ
Ul'yanovsk Motor Vehicle Plant, Ul'yanovsk, USSR

UMM
Umm-Uniao Metalo-Mecanica Lda., Rua des Flores, Lisbon, Portugal

VOLKSWAGEN
Volkswagen AG, Wolfsburg, Germany

Engineering, 94: Lohr Industries, 96: Mercedes-Benz, 97: Mercedes-Benz, 98–99: Julian McNamara, 101 (both pictures): Mitsubishi/Colt UK, 102–103: Julian McNamara, 104: Nissan, 105: Nissan, 106–107: Dangel, 109: Bart Vanderveen, 110–111: Portaro, 113: SIMI, 114–115: Renault, 116: SIMI, 117: Sbarro, 118–119: Sbarro, 120–121: Bart Vanderveen, 122: Steyr-Daimler-Puch, 123: Subaru, 124–125: Subaru, 125: Suzuki, 128–129 (all pictures): Suzuki, 130: Suzuki, 131: Julian McNamara, 132: Julian McNamara, 133: Toyota, 134: Toyota, 136–137: Toyota, 139 (all pictures): Toyota, 140–141: Toyota, 142: Bart Vanderveen, 143: Julian McNamara, 144–145: Bart Vanderveen, 146: Bart Vanderveen, 147: Bombardier, 149 /top): VAG, 149 (below): Bombardier, 150: VAG Endpapers: Rich Johnson

A1173